Stardust In Dixie

By

Beth Albright

STARDUST IN DIXIE
© Copyright 2016 Magnolia Press
ALL RIGHTS RESERVED

ISBN: 978-0-9913698-5-0

Awards & Accolades for author Beth Albright

DOUBLE Finalist for the **RT REVIEWERS Awards**

The Sassy Belles for *BEST CONTEMPORARY ROMANCE*

Wedding Belles for *BEST Contemporary Love and Laughter*

The Sassy Belles WINNER: *Best Debut Novel* from the *Book Junkie Choice Awards*

The Sassy Belles—
*Finalist BEST DEBUT NOVEL, RT REVIEWERS AWARDS, 2014
*Top Five Summer Pick – Deep South Magazine
*Finalist: Best Debut Novel – Book Junkie Choice Awards

Wedding Belles—
*Finalist BEST NOVEL, LOVE AND LAUGHTER, RT REVIEWERS AWARDS 2014
*RT Magazine Top Pick for August
*Nominated for GOLD SEAL OF EXCELLENCE, RT Magazine/August

Sleigh Belles—
*Barnes and Noble Bookseller Picks: September Top Pick for Romance

Praise For The Novels of Beth Albright

- Dripping with southern charm and colloquialisms, the novel once again proves Albright's firsthand knowledge of southern culture. *The women in Albright's novels are especially well written*—happy to challenge the status quo when necessary but also aware of that old adage, "You catch more flies with honey." This delightfully campy and romantic read will satisfy fans of Mary Kay Andrews, Alexandra Potter, and Lisa Jewell. **Booklist Review for** *Wedding Belles*

- *By turns tender, witty, steamy, and sharp, Albright's debut novel proves she's a gifted storyteller* with intimate knowledge of southern culture. This charming tale is tailor-made for fans of Mary Kay Andrews and Anne George." –**Booklist Review for** *The Sassy Belles*

- *...with distinct nods to the strength of family, the friendship sisterhood and the indomitable Southern spirit...Albright's first novel is a frothy, frolicking story..."* –**Kirkus Review for** *The Sassy Belles*

- *"Albright good-naturedly displays her inner redneck while steering this giddy Dixie romp with ease-leaving lots of room at the happy ending for another adventure starring these steel magnolias"* – **Publisher's Weekly Review for** *The Sassy Belles*

- "Readers will find some sexy, Southern fun for Christmas with The Sassy Belles." – Library Journal for *Sleigh Belles*

- *"The Sassy Belles are back and sassier than ever! ... With clever dialogue and richly drawn characters, Albright shows once again she's a natural-born storyteller who knows how to pen a charming tale.* Regardless of game-day colors worn, this sexy and fun Southern series will have readers coming back for more!" –**RT Magazine Review for** *Wedding Belles*

- *"The Sassy Belles reminded me that the South is like no other place on earth. Kudos to Beth Albright for capturing its spirit so perfectly in this lighthearted debut novel."* -Celia Rivenbark, New York Times bestselling author of *We're Just Like You, Only Prettier*

- *" Magic In Dixie serves up a heaping helping of Southern flavor and humor sure to please. Known for writing memorable characters with true southern voices and mannerisms, Albright ensures you don't have to be born in the south to appreciate the charm of her latest. So grab a box of Krispy Kreme doughnuts—you'll devour them as easily as this enjoyable summer read."* – RT BookReviews

- *"Beth Albright knocks it out of the ballpark with Christmas In Dixie. The characters are fun and full of life. What a great read!"*— BookMamaBlog

Other Novels By Beth Albright

In Dixie Series:

Magic In Dixie (Book One)

Christmas In Dixie (Book Two)

Daydreams In Dixie (Book Three)

The Sassy Belles Series:

The Sassy Belles

Wedding Belles

Sleigh Belles

Saved By The Belles

Memoirs

Southern Exposure; Tales From My Front Porch

Coming in 2016:

Southern Comfort; A Southern Girl's Guide to Cooking

Jingle Belles In Dixie

Dedication:

To one of my favorite people on earth, my Aunt Patricia Catherine Bruce, (Patsy) Your sunny, positive influence has helped shape my life. I was always so proud when Mother would tell me, "You are just like your Aunt Patsy!" It would take an entire book to tell you all you have meant to me my whole life. You always showered me with love and happiness and so much fun and laughter—you are a huge part of who I am. And I couldn't be prouder. I am so glad we have each other! Thank you for always helping me to spread the word about my books!! And for always letting me know how proud you are of me! I love you.

And, as always to my son, my sweetheart, Brooks, my patient, loving, husband, Ted, and my precious mother, Betty— And to one of my biggest supporters, my stepfather of over 35 years, Richard J. Spavins—y'all are my universe. Where would I be without y'all? I love you all so very much.

Thank you so much to the beautiful Randa DeLane Simpson. I am so honored to have your stunning image grace my cover.

And to the talented photographer, Sydney Broadaway Meeks, for this fabulous one-of-a- kind shot. I am the luckiest author ever!

CHAPTER ONE

I don't know what finally made me snap that day—what finally made me do what I did. I still don't know. Something finally pushed me over the edge. And I'm not like that. I'm the calm one. The one who's always in control. My sisters both pitch hissy fits weekly. I have never thrown one in public—until today. Today was different. After years of irritation, competition, and frustration, I just finally snapped. The frustration just began to bubble and I knew I would blow if just one more thing piled up on me. So, before I made a big scene, which I have never done. I left. I left my desk a wreck, I didn't say goodbye to my sister and I stormed out the office door and jumped in my car and sped out of the parking lot, the gravel and rocks spewing up behind me. All I could think as I shoved the accelerator to the floor was that man—that unbelievable man! Ugh! He had finally pushed me off the edge and the pressure just finally got to me. I wasn't even sure I wanted to come back to work—ever!

My name is Abigail Harper. I'm the Promotions Director at WRCT in Tuscaloosa Alabama. My sister is a talk show host here. Annabelle Harper is actually my twin though we look nothing alike. And we sure don't act anything alike. She is all beauty, boobs and drama. I look like Princess Kate. I act more like her too—dignified and in control. Except for today.

This thing with Greg had been going on for nearly a month. Well, he had been competitive with me for as long as I could remember. But this intense amount of pressure was new. Greg Galloway had been a pain in my side since we were in college, both of us majoring in Public Relations at The University of Alabama. He was competitive to a fault—always had to be on top, always doing anything he had to, even playing dirty, paying people off, so he could be on top. Stealing my promotions idea, and even paying spokespeople out of his own pocket so he could steal them from me. He worked as the PR Director at a competing radio station. And once again, here was Greg, making me crazy. I seriously believe he has a mole planted at our station. I think of a huge promotion for our hosts, and the next thing you know, before I can pull it off, WRBI is beating me to the punch. He was exactly the same in college. He peered over my shoulder in every exam. Spied on me as I created my projects in the lab. Planted people near me so they would "overhear" my ideas I'd share with my student teams. He has always known I am better, more creative, more outspoken and certainly much more focused than he'd ever be. But today—today was different. I felt like steam was coming out of my ears. It was the final straw and I swear, I had visions of me literally strangling him. I was fuming as I sped out onto 15th Street and headed to anywhere but near a radio station. I was tired. I was angry. But I knew even though I was ready to quit, in the end all I really wanted to do was win; beat Greg Galloway at his own game.

I found myself sitting outside Reese Phifer Hall on the University campus. It housed the School Of Communications. No idea why I drove there. It was where this relationship with Greg Galloway began. It was like I wanted to start over, nip it in the bud. I sat still in my car, looking around at the regal campus and historic old building. A wave of memories washed over me as I felt the tears well and sting my eyes. This place held some of my favorite memories even though Greg had been such a huge part of my life back then. My mind began to wander as the afternoon sun peeked through the two-hundred year old oaks, the shadows from the green leaves dancing in speckled shapes over the old columns at the top of the stairs.

It was late spring and the summer was teasing us, dodging behind the rain clouds that usually hovered in the late afternoon skies. But today was warm and humid with cornflower blue skies. I gazed up at the top of the stairs. Suddenly it was freshman year and I was a Phi Mu pledge, my long dark brown hair pulled back away from my face. My blue eyes filled with excitement and hope as the year began.

Then I met him. Sitting behind me in PR101 was the most beautiful man, dark brown eyes and dark blonde hair swept deep to the side, golden strands hanging loosely over his tanned forehead. He was all prepped out in Ralph Lauren and Polo, Topsiders without socks. He had on light gray shorts with a baby blue polo shirt. With his perfect white teeth and deep dimples, he looked like a model. He slid into his desk right behind me and I felt my heart quicken. He leaned forward and whispered to me.

"Hey, I'm Greg. What's your name?" I grinned to myself, filled with nerves and giddiness. I leaned backwards to answer him.

"I'm Abby. Hey." My heart nearly thumping right out of my chest.

The professor came in and class began, but I couldn't pay a bit of attention. All I could think of was that delicious man behind me. Within a week, Greg and I were studying together. Well we called it studying, but mostly we were kissing. He was such a smooth operator. Get this—one night we were studying and he was talking about his drama class and how he had a kissing scene coming up.

"I don't know this girl and really it makes me a little nervous," he said.

"Uh huh, I bet," I smirked. I knew Greg was too cool, too easy to have nerves about anything, especially kissing a random girl. I was pretty sure he specialized in that—kissing random girls.

"No, seriously. I'm a little nervous I might make a fool of

myself. But I think you can help me." Greg steadied his gaze.

"Oh really? I teased. "And just what do you need me to do?"

"Come over here," he motioned. "Sit next to me."

I got up from my desk and slowly approached Greg. He was sitting on the side of his bed. Greg had an apartment and was a year older than me. It was dusk, the sun had set, autumn leaves drifted down to the damp ground past his windowsill. Twilight slipped through the curtains as I sat down next to him, our thighs touching. It was late September in Alabama and that particular night it was unseasonably warm. The heat was sultry, both outside—and inside. My heartbeat quickened.

"I have an idea," he began. "Maybe if I kiss you, it would make me more comfortable when I'm doin' my scene in class tomorrow."

"So you want to practice the scene with me?" I asked coyly.

"Or we can write our own script," he whispered. Greg looked up at me from under those thick dark blonde bangs and slowly moved his head closer, tilting it sideways. He teased me, his breath on my mouth. He held back making me crazed with excitement. Closer he came until his soft warm lips rested upon mine. He didn't move them at first—just letting them get familiar with mine. Then as he moved his lips in a slow rhythm, I felt myself lose all awareness. The room began spinning. Greg was the most gorgeous man I had ever laid eyes on, let alone kissed. I was lost. I felt myself slipping down the side of the bed as Greg leaned further and further over me. I hit the floor with a thud.

"Oh my God, I am so sorry!" I giggled. Greg slid off and landed next to me.

"You are adorable," he laughed. "Kiss me again." Greg kissed me harder and as his mouth wandered on mine, I felt heat rise all over me for the first time in my life. Greg was warm and funny and soft and sexy. It had only been a couple of weeks of practicing for his drama class and knew I was falling hard for him. Little did I know by the time college was over, Greg Galloway would become enemy number one.

CHAPTER TWO

I sat in my car lost in memories until dusk began to fall. Suddenly the doors to Reese Phifer swung open and a tall slender but well built man with dark wavy hair emerged. He was dressed in a baby blue button-down and light kakis. He looked as delicious as he did our senior year. I recognized him right away. Ben Flannigan was everything Greg Galloway wasn't. And he saved me from him all those years ago. What had I done by turning him down that summer after graduation? I almost never forgave myself. Looking at him now as he began to descend the stairs of the regal old building, his books tucked under his arm, his tan skin making those blue eyes match the periwinkle skies, I felt a sadness begin to bubble up in my throat. He was once almost mine. But I let him go.

I had no idea he was even still in town. Once I turned down his proposal, he disappeared from my life. He was an old soul and I knew that from the moment I met him. It was what had attracted me to him. He was calm and centered and soothing. His deep voice was slow and unhurried. He wasn't a party-goer—not too much of a drinker. He loved nights in, ordering Chinese food and snuggling up—with me. We got together the summer before our senior year working at an internship in town. Then we worked on our capstone project all year together, spending hours and hours talking and laughing and creating such great work. All the while, Greg Galloway tried everything he could to undermine us on every single level. Ben and I became a team working against Greg. It was bonding. By year's end we were so deeply in love and the old soul in him wanted nothing but to settle down with me and get married. I just wasn't ready.

It's been nearly fourteen years. I had heard he was engaged at one time. I think that was a while ago.

Just then he glanced up. I was staring at him as he bounced down the stairs and he stopped when he saw me watching him. I was certain I looked like a stalker. Like I had come there just to look for him, like I knew his schedule. I was mortified. He squinted as if he wasn't sure it was me. He grinned and headed over to my little white BMW. My heart raced as I hit the button, my window going down, losing the barrier between us. I swallowed hard as he approached, my heart jumping as he came closer. What would I say after all these years? I had no idea. The break-up was beyond awful. Before I could think of a single thing to utter, he was at my window.

"Hey Abby. Long time, huh?" He grinned that perfect smile, framed by a single dimple on his left cheek; his deep set blue eyes sparkled, framed by thick dark lashes too long to belong to a man.

"Hey yourself," I smiled, my racing heart nearly choking me.

"What are you doing here?" he asked still grinning.

"Uhm, well, I uhm, just went for a drive and ended up here." I sounded like an idiot.

Ben smiled and touched my shoulder. He was just the same, trying to put me at ease. The caregiver. I suddenly found it strange that I was in the same situation sitting here in my car—that Greg had driven me to the brink, and Ben was ready to soothe my frustrations. It was just like senior year all over again.

"What are you doing here?" I asked. I mean we sure weren't in college any more yet here he was, with books under his arm.

"Oh, I work here now. I'm a professor," he smiled.

"What? You're teaching?" I know I sounded like a fool. Of course he was teaching, I thought. He said he was a professor! My end of this awkward conversation was going down in flames.

"Yes, I am. Is that so unbelievable?" he chortled.

"Oh no, not at all. I guess I just didn't even know you were still in town. Now that I think about it, professor just makes perfect sense," I chattered.

"Well, I hope that's a complement." He grinned just enough for me to see that single left dimple.

"So what are you up to these days? Still at WRCT?" He continued.

"How did you know I worked there?"

"Oh well, I uhm, just knew. I mean Tuscaloosa isn't that big you know?" Ben mused.

"Yeah, that's true," I agreed. I knew he must be keeping up with me. I was ashamed I hadn't kept up with him.

"What made you drive over here? Were you coming to see someone about a promotion?" he asked.

I hesitated for a split second, looking up at him.

"Abby? Is something going on?" He was always so intuitive.

"No, not really. Why?" I responded trying to fake a smile.

Ben squatted down next to the car. With his tall frame we were suddenly face-to- face. I wished I had my sunglasses. As close as we were now, I knew he would be able to see I had been crying.

"Come on Abby. I know you. Even after all these years, I can tell. Plus you have mascara smeared on your cheek here." He touched my face softly. "I don't have to be a genius to know something has upset you," he said sweetly. "I also know you don't just drive aimlessly somewhere unless you needed to get away from something. Things aren't adding up. So tell me? Let me see if I can help."

I drew in a deep breath. I felt like I was 21 again. "Okay. Just get in." It was like no time had passed. Like one of those friendships that when you bump into that person, you just talk and the time in between evaporates. As Ben made his way around the car I realized this was exactly what I needed. No one I knew understood the situation with Greg like he did. No one could understand how all this incredible frustration, for years and years now, could possibly cause me to break like I did today. Only Ben. He had been through it with me before. He opened the door and slid onto my tan leather seats bringing his long legs under the dash and shut the door.

"Okay spill," he demanded. "I'm here and nothing you say is going anywhere. Just let me help you if I can." He looked deeply at me. Ben knew me so well. And it sure seemed he hadn't forgotten a thing. I was almost always fully in control of myself. I was slightly, well almost totally a perfectionist and a major clean-freak. I would go as far as to say I was possibly an OCD clean freak. If someone set their glass down and didn't touch it for 60 seconds, it was in in the dishwasher.

"Look, seriously," I explained. "I don't want to hold you up. It looked like you were in a hurry—anyway, it's nothing new."

"I wasn't in a big hurry. I was just headed up to my parents. One of the horses may be headed for the derby this year. It's a long shot but they have some meetings this weekend and they wanted me to be in on them. I can drive home tonight, no big deal."

Ben's family owned Flannigan Farms in North Alabama. He had grown up around race horses all of his life. They bred them and sold them.

"Is Annie okay? Is it your crazy mother? Come on, Abby. Let me help if I can," he pushed softly.

"Okay, well this will be no surprise to you, of all people. It's Greg. He's been at it again for a month. I have planned one promotion after the next, weekend after weekend and he's beaten me to the punch every single time. He's stealing our sponsors left and right and today he scored a huge one. I swear I just can't take it one more time. He's exactly the same as he was when we knew him in class." I felt fresh tears sting my eyes. "I don't know, maybe I'm just tired."

"Look at me Abby," he said. "You are better than Greg Galloway any day of the week. You know that. That idiot never had an original idea of his own from day one. He had to steal all of his projects from you. You're the creative one. You always were."

"I'm just at a loss. I mean I think someone in the station is spying for him."

"Of course they are. That was always his way. Remember when he sent Jamie Thompson to join our team and she was being paid by him to steal our ideas? It's always been his way. That is the only reason he's gotten as far as he has. Now all you need to do is find out who the spy is. Catch them at their own game." Ben stopped for a moment. I could tell he was thinking.

"What? What is it?"

"I'm just thinking maybe I could help. I have student interns over at Greg's station. Let me think over the weekend and maybe I could call you next week."

"Oh that sounds great," I smiled feeling somewhat relieved.

Ben looked better than he even did in college. He was a man now, fleshed out with more end of the day stubble than he had back then. I felt so badly about how it all had ended. Just then I felt his hand rest on mine. He gave it a gentle squeeze. I was taken aback by his touch, though it was familiar, it wasn't the same. He pressed his lips together in a knowing smile. "It'll be Okay, Abby. Promise."

"Thanks," I managed. I felt so awkward. The last time Ben and I saw each other was when we were breaking up. Now here we were nearly 14 years later, and it felt like no time had passed. But it had. I had a fleeting thought that he might be married. A guy as gorgeous as he was surely was taken by now, I thought. I glanced down at his left hand on mine. Nope, no ring. Maybe he was divorced. I was racking my brain trying to remember that girl he was engaged to. What the hell was her name? Oh, Colleen Cantrell. Right. I had to know what happened. I swallowed and squeezed his hand back and looked up at him.

"Thanks for helping me, I mean offering to help me," I stumbled. "I hope no one is waiting for you somewhere because of me," I pried.

"No, just my family up north."

"Anyone going with you?" I pushed a little more.

"Come on Abby, just ask me. You wanna know if there's a better half? No, not anymore. I mean you knew about Colleen, right?"

"Yeah, I did. I thought you two were engaged for a while."

"We were. The engagement lasted about two years. It finally ended as the wedding plans were in motion, the exact day the invitations arrived to be exact."

"Oh Ben, I'm so sorry," I interrupted.

"I dated a couple of other women here and there but nothing ever came of any of it."

"Didn't you date Colleen for like three years before you finally popped the question? Looks like she would have known whether she wanted to marry you long before the wedding date was nearly here."

"You mean like you did?"

Ouch. "Okay I can take it. I know I hurt you. I didn't mean to. I just, wasn't ready. I mean we were so young, Ben. I'm still so sorry about it all."

"Well, I didn't *feel* young. I felt in love and I knew what I wanted. But hey, that was a long time ago, right? What about you? Anybody in your life these days?"

"No, not anyone right now. I went through a pretty bad relationship a few years ago but nothing too recent."

There was that little affair two years ago. It was short-lived but heavy. I didn't want to say anything to make Ben feel bad so I tried to brush it off. I should have known better.

"Didn't you have a little thing a couple of years ago? I actually heard you were seeing Greg for a while. Was that true? I'd swear that was what I heard but I never believed it. I know how you hated him in college."

What Ben didn't know was that Greg was my first. A heated night during sophomore year, Greg's commanding presence, his persuasive voice and all of that insatiable affection, I found him completely irresistible. All he had to do was give me a look, a wink and I was gone. And I have such a love- hate relationship with him. When Greg is good he's the sexiest man I have ever known, and when he is bad, I hate him to his core. Somehow he has always been able to sweet talk his was back into my life. I'm the idiot who falls for him every single time. Looks like I would have learned. It took me a while but I finally did. *Never again*, I told myself. He is an ass with a capital A. Always has been and always would be.

My relationship with Ben was much sweeter. He was gentle and treated me with such love and care. Such deep devotion. He was unlike any man I had ever known. I was a fool back then when I turned him down but I was young and pretty stupid.

"Oh, yeah, well, I am really an idiot sometimes," I readily admitted. "It was only a month or so. Didn't take me long to learn that one of us had grown up and it wasn't Greg. I ended it pretty fast." I tried to blow it off but Ben continued.

"Yeah, I couldn't believe it when I heard. I knew you must have lost your mind."

"I did. That's for sure." I looked away hoping to change the subject fast. He could tell the moment had become awkward.

"Well, just know I'm here for you, Abby. You have never been a person to fall apart. I always admired your strength. All of this will be okay. I'll think about it all weekend. Maybe we can get together for coffee sometime next week."

"Sure. I would really appreciate that," I said hopefully.

Ben grabbed the door handle and turned to get out of the car. I found myself not wanting him to go.

"Ben, I'm so glad I ran into you," I added quickly.

"Yeah, me too Abby. It was really good seeing you. Are you sure you weren't stalking me?"

"No, but it's funny, I needed a safe place to hide for a few hours and you were my harbor tonight. Funny," I suddenly realized. "Some things just never change."

G'night Abby. I'll call you next week."

"Okay. Drive safe." I offered.

Ben shut the car door. He glanced back over his shoulder and gave me a wave. Ben was a comfort, a port in the storm. The question was, could he ever really forgive me for what I did to him all those years ago?

CHAPTER THREE

I drove into my driveway at a crawl. My head was spinning. I had thought about Ben here and there over the years but never seriously. I knew I didn't stand a chance of ever being with him again. It wasn't that I didn't love him. I did. I just didn't want to get married—not then. I had hurt him so badly and yet, today, he seemed like he had forgotten it all—or at least he had forgiven me, after I had humiliated him in front of his entire family. I never thought for a second I'd ever have another chance with him, and maybe I don't. Maybe he was just being Ben today, sweet and loving and good no matter what.

Years ago, when he proposed to me, Ben had gone all out with his elaborate plans. He obviously had been planning it for months, saving every dime he had made from working at a pizza place at night, and bought me the most stunning ring I had ever seen. He was so certain I would say yes. The thing was, we had talked about marriage. A lot. I loved Ben. I was sure of that. It was such a strong healthy relationship. So different from the one I had with Greg.

Greg was all hot and lust and racing hearts. I did care so much for him too, but with Ben it was different. It was a grown-up kind of love. We were friends, partners, and lovers.

He was my very best friend. We were inseparable. It had been like that for nearly a year. We hadn't spent even one day apart. I moved in with him for our senior year. We scheduled our classes together, we cooked, we went grocery shopping. It was what seemed like married life. It was the most intense relationship I had ever had with anyone. I never thought for a second we wouldn't get married—one day. Ben was perfect husband material. So strong—a natural leader, though he was so gentle and sweet. I could lean on him in ways I had never known before. I was usually the one in control but with Ben I could finally relax and take a deep breath and let someone else drive, so to speak.

Ben had taken me out to Lake Tuscaloosa the summer after graduation from the University of Alabama. Both of us had just landed jobs here in town and we knew one day we would get married. It was just an understood fact between us. But for my old soul Ben Flannigan, that day came sooner than later. And much sooner than *I* had planned. Ben had hired a long distance photographer, you know those hidden photographers with the zoom lens that can capture candid moments from hundreds of feet away. His family and my family were all hiding around a park when we got to a gazebo on his family's property. He helped me out of the boat and walked me up to the rose and ivy covered trellis near the lakeshore and before I knew it he had dropped to one knee. My stomach dropped right with him. I was dumbfounded. I felt like I couldn't breathe.

"I love you Abby. I have loved you since I laid eyes on you two years ago. I know there's so much we have to learn. I know so many people have said we're too young. But I know us. And that's what makes it all okay. It's you and me. I feel safe in your arms and I know you are safe in mine. I'm sure you are who I want to spend the rest of my life with. As long as we're together, everything will be just fine. I know it. Abigail Harper Cartwright, will you make me the happiest man on earth and do me the honor of marrying me?"

I felt like I was being strangled. I covered my mouth with my trembling hands and the tears gushed over the rims of my emotional eyes. Before I could answer, the entire family burst out from the bushes and ran toward us. Ben was still on one knee. I began to shake my head uncontrollably.

"Ben, I can't. I'm...I'm...just not ready to be married. I love you so much but can't we wait a while? I mean, we're so young and we have so many things we want to do." I was mumbling though shaky words and falling tears and a massive lump in my throat. Ben stood up and heaved in a deep breath—humiliated. "Abby, I love you. And I know you love me."

The families could barely make out what was happening with all the excitement. Then Ben shouted, "She said no." He rose to his feet, still holding the ring and walked away in shame, his head hanging down; he looked at no one as he made his way up to the lake house. His parents went running after him. I burst into tears, shaking and crying uncontrollably, running as far as I could until no one could hear my sobs. What had I done?

I tried to shake the memories as I sat in my car in the driveway—darkness had fallen an hour ago. I was trying to process the details of what was happening. Or happening again. It felt like an echo of my past, shadows of life as it was before the terrible mistake I had made with Ben, and the bigger mistake that followed with Greg. Here both of these men were again, back in my life in the same roles they had played on this stage before. We were all such different people now, but so much the same. Back then we had no idea what life would bring us. Our youthful conversations devoid of life's uncertainty, we had the future by the tale. We didn't know we were standing on the precipice, of a life-change that would grab all of us and shake us as we headed full frontal into the unknown. We didn't know we stood on the brink; instead we felt as if we skipped along the rocky shores, so optimistic of our footsteps, certain of sunshine and so thirsty for the new chapters of our unwritten stories to unfold. Our lifetimes stretched out to the bright horizons in front of us, pulling at us to believe there was still so much time. And all of our futures lay ahead, glistening with promise and boundless with possibility. But life hardly ever turns out to match our imaginations. And now, here we are, our lives again crisscrossing on the same worn paths as before, so long ago.

I heaved in a deep breath and got out of my car. Annie, my twin sister, had moved out when she and her new fiancé, Matt Brubaker, got their own place last fall. I now lived alone in the same old craftsman near the center of town. I made my way up the cracked sidewalk to the wide front porch and pushed my key into the front door, slipping inside to the dark empty house. As the front door opened and a note dropped to the floor. It had been stuffed into my screened door.

Dearest Abby, I declare you are such a dear. Thank you so much for leaving that beautiful basket of Azaleas on my porch as a 'welcome to the neighborhood' gift. While the flowers were beautiful and the candy and fruits were so thoughtful, as a new life coach, I am now on a gluten free, fructose free meal plan. I appreciate the gesture. Oh, I am allergic to Azaleas, so if you don't mind, would you be a doll and remove the bushes in the shared alley-way?
Thanks so much,
Mitzy McDonald.

I slammed my front door. I knew I would never like that over made-up sorority slut. All my dreamy memories evaporated in an instant. I was already so upset by Greg that day. I could barely keep myself from marching next door and telling her off!

Just then the phone rang. I grabbed the receiver on the counter as I entered the kitchen.

"Hey darlin' you gonna make it to Book Club tonight? We're all gonna make up fake names and pretend it's the 20s. You sure won't wanna miss that now!"

Sigh. "Nope I would never want to miss that fake name

thing," I answered back. The book club president on the other end of the line giggled. Dixie Darlene Holifield was just what you would imagine, round and as loud as a T-Rex in a grocery store with a giggle you would recognize a mile away, which always ended in a snort. I had forgotten the Book Club tonight but the new identity was surely intriguing.

"Sure, honey, count me in," I agreed.

"Fab sugar! See you in an hour!" Dixie hung up.

I shook my head as I grabbed the white wine from the fridge. A Zinfandel, I pried the cork and swigged it right from the bottle. Gertrude my oversized fat gray cat came waddling into the kitchen and let out a slow meow. It was as if she needed a swig too. I poured her food and scratched her back before I headed upstairs to grab a light sundress and my white sweater. It was a sultry night, the crickets and fireflies in rhythm with the evening's outdoor symphony. I hated to admit it, but I hadn't even started the new book yet. I knew I could fake it. Plus, knowing Dixie, she'd have Krispy Kremes and mimosas waiting. I moved a little faster, stepping back out on my front porch and locking the door behind me.

Just as I turned, I tripped over the basket of azaleas. Mitzy had returned them due to her allergies, but of course, she appreciated the gesture. *Is this really my life?* I thought. I trodded to the car and slid into the driver's seat. Mimosas fried sugar and a fake name sure sounded like just what I needed tonight!

CHAPTER FOUR

I didn't remember much about Book Club as the sun peeked through the pale blue sheers over my bedroom windows. It was Saturday and I had slept in. The mimosas were talking to me all night. Along with me seeing Ben's gorgeous face every time I closed my eyes, I barely slept a wink. I was restless until nearly dawn then slept like a baby. It was just after 10AM as I stretched and drew in a deep breath. I stumbled into the bathroom and glanced at my face in the mirror. Zelda. That was my Book Club name. I drew the name Fannie, like Fannie Bryce. But I told Dixie I was changing it. I wanted to be Zelda. The truly talented one, the one who fought her way to the bitter end, the one who didn't take shit from anybody. Today, I could see Zelda staring back at me. Well, at least I could adopt her as my muse until she emerged more clearly. I had been calm for too long, controlled and organized and always doing the right thing for far too long. I needed a new way of living. I felt like I needed a little crazy.

I stepped into the shower and began to think. Never a good thing after three too many drinks. Today was the day. Greg Galloway was putting on the promotion of the season, the one he had stolen from me a month ago. He had the Alabama quarterback in the center ring of his media circus. He stole him too. He got to him first. We had a big fundraiser planned, had booked sponsors, secured the venue and boom—Greg Galloway strikes again. I didn't want to go *anywhere* near the campus today. That event was going on and I knew it would make me infuriated. But my curiosity was getting the best of me.

I turned around in the oversized shower, the hot water massaging my aching head. The fixtures had all been updated in the 1920's little bathroom, but we kept all the original charm. We even left some of the pink tiles here and there amid the slick white subway tiles. It was beautiful. The phone in my bedroom was ringing just as I stepped out. I wrapped my long brunette hair in a blush pink towel, threw on my white robe and headed back to my bedroom. It was my sister, Annie.

"Hey honey, so you going out to spy on WRBI today?"

"I really don't want to…"

"But…?" She interrupted.

Nothing. I'm just curious."

"Let's go! Matt is out of town and I'm ready to be naughty. Well, you know what I mean. Hey maybe we can get some ideas, look around the crowd, see if we recognize someone who might be his spy. You know what?"

"What Annie?" I was afraid to ask.

"Maybe we can beat that Greg at his own game. Let's go get into some trouble over there! Don't you think he'll wonder what we're doing there?"

"Okay you got me. Give me a half hour and come get me."

I hung up and headed into my walk-in closet to get ready. We had knocked an older smaller bedroom out and created a dressing room right out of a fairy-tale. I had my vanity table and a covered footstool in the middle. My clothes hung all around. Suits. I suddenly realized more work clothes surrounded me than fun clothes. It made me cringe. I sat down in the Queen Anne mint and white striped upholstered chair and stared at myself in the mirror as I hurriedly applied my make-up, the brushes caressing my face. Who was that looking back at me? I had become a work-a-holic. A lonely work-a-holic. For years after my last romp with Greg I could count the number of dates I had gone with one hand, and I didn't even need the whole hand. It was pathetic. I finished my face and grabbed a swingy white skirt, the only skirt I had that was *swingy*. I dug until I found a pair of flat sandals, and a pink tank top, along with a Lilly Pulitzer pink and green paisley cardigan. I needed a change. I felt lighter with the clothes on but still so nervous about running into Greg.

I heard Annie honk and hurried down the stairs, patting Gertrude on her back. Perched on the back of the couch, she stretched in the sunshine that was streaming through the front windows as I locked the front door.

"Hey girlie, look at you!" Annie yelled from her car.

"What?" I questioned nonchalantly as I tried to play it down.

"You—you look adorable."

Was that the look I was going for?

"I mean seriously Abby, I know that drab predictable wardrobe you have. Where did you dig this up from, your college collection? *My* leftovers in my room?"

I got in and shut the door and stared at her. "Okay, okay, I get it. I just wanted to feel less serious today. So I added in some color, that's all."

"Well, I for one, love it," Annie popped. "Especially since this may be the first time in almost ten years you aren't wearing black or navy or crimson—your signature drab colors." She laughed as she backed out, her little convertible spitting gravel as we headed left down the tree-tunneled street. Mitzy was sweeping her porch and glanced up at the noise and waved a half-assed wave.

I sat in the front seat quietly as we drove. My thoughts swirled to Ben as my gut clenched thinking of Greg. I decided to tell Annie about running into Ben.

"Guess who sat in my car last night," I said.

"Well since you have totally changed your appearance,

I'm gonna guess your fairy Godmother?"

No Miss Priss, you are going to be even more surprised—Ben Flannigan.

"Oh my word, Abby! Did y'all have a date?"

"No, I was out near the Communications School and I saw him coming down the stairs. He saw me and came over to the car."

"And he got in? Wow sure looks like he doesn't hold a grudge after all these years. You know, after you humiliated him in front of God and everybody," she smirked.

"Thanks for the sweet subtle reminder. What a dear you are."

"Anyway so go ahead. Why was he in your car?"

"I was pretty upset yesterday. Greg stole another promotion. I was working on it yesterday and called to confirm and they said it had been double booked. I asked and it was him, of course. "

"Oh God! What is wrong with that asshole? He has no mind of his own. Never has. What was it?"

"An event I wanted to do to kick off May over Mother's Day weekend. I wanted to use the old Jemison Van de Graff Mansion. I was planning to throw an old fashioned summer social, with the men in seersucker, you know."

"And what? Greg took your location—again?"

"Yep. It's booked. By WRBI for Mother's Day."

"Okay fine!" Annie popped.

"What do you mean *Fine*?" I asked.

"Just book the Battle Friedman Home. It will be hilarious. It's right across the street. Call them right now. I bet they're open. Just book it and we'll figure out the rest later."

I didn't even stop to argue with her. If she was ready to go to war with Greg then great, we would. I had back-up—my twin sister. I called them and booked the date. They had just had a wedding cancellation that morning. It was sad that the bride had to cancel her wedding but great for me.

"Okay we got it. I can't believe it at this late date too! It's just a few weeks."

"Wonderful, we'll beat that ass at his own game, you'll see. So go ahead now, why was Ben in your car? Did he kiss you?"

"Oh my Lord, Annie! No he did not. You are so hopeless."

"It's how I make my living remember? As a hopeless romantic."

Annie hosted a radio show at the station. It was called *Saved By The Belle*, a romance show where she helps people find their long lost loves.

"Of course but Ben would never kiss me after what happened, I mean it will be a miracle if we can just be friends."

"So again, he was in your car, and…" She pushed.

"Yes, he came down the steps and saw me. I had been so mad I had been crying and I was just sitting there. He got in to cheer me up."

"And did he?" She asked with a drawl and a wink.

"Annie I swear you don't have to keep doing your show with me. I am fine. Ben and I will be friends. He offered to help me with Greg."

"Oh, I bet he did." Annie grinned as we drove the shady warm streets of Tuscaloosa. The Magnolias were abloom everywhere I looked. The sweet fragrances enveloped me as we rode along past all the old homes, the historic romance of this old wonderful town held me in its arms. I wasn't sure if all these hopeful feelings were coming from my lighter outfit, the fact that I now had two partners to help me go after Greg, or just Ben Flannigan himself stepping back into my life. But one thing was for sure—*Zelda* had certainly arrived!

CHAPTER FIVE

We pulled into a tree-covered spot near the Gorgas House on campus. Suddenly flashes of Ben and me kissing on the upstairs porch of the historic home on campus late one night began floating around in my mind. I was lost in the memory when Annie grabbed my arm.

"Oh God, honey, there he is."

"Who?" I looked up and away from the Gorgas House only to see Greg Galloway getting out of his silver Mercedes. The anger rose in me. I felt steam rise up and nearly choke me. I wanted to beat him, not just at his own game but with the business end of a shovel. I knew this time was different. He had set up so many similar promotions and I could never prove he was planting spies at our station, but this time, he grabbed the same person I was trying to book for the very same event, one to help the Children's Museum with summer programs. I had tried to overlook things in the past, even forgiving him, giving into his charming ways, but this time I knew he was using me. He had probably always been using me. Of course he had, what was I thinking?

"Okay look Abby, we need to make a plan. He will be smug, you can guarantee it. He'll want to know why we're here but you know he'll make it like we just couldn't stay away from this fabulous event. He will be his usual pompous blowhard self. We have to end things by leaving him guessing. I'll take the lead. You just follow me. You are too emotional right now. Honey, I can't believe I just said that. That may be the first time anyone has ever called you too emotional. It may be that skirt, but I am pretty sure it's Mr. Ben Flannigan." She grinned at me as we headed over to the Quad, falling in right next to Greg.

"Well, well, hello lovely ladies. I can't believe my eyes. What are you two doing here? Spying?"

God he was an ass.

"Why yes, how did you ever guess? No really we're here to meet my other sister down on the strip. We just thought we'd walk since it's such a lovely day."

Annie was good.

"Yes, Rhonda is here somewhere," I added.

"Really? Well you're missing out on the event of the spring. Y'all come on over and say hi to Jake Coker. He's a dynamite of a player. He's just over there near the Ferris wheel signing autographs for the Children's Museum. "

Oh I was squirming inside. I wanted to hit him right that second. He knew I had planned to book Jake. Somehow he found out and got to him before I could. I was supposed to be spending *my* Saturday with Jake Coker. Ugh I was so mad I could spit nails but I couldn't let Greg see that. I had to stay calm and unaffected. Greg knew what he had done, and he knew that I knew. But if I looked like I was upset he had won. So I just smiled.

"Oh he knows me," I said of Jake Coker. "I met him last year during the season. The station had sideline passes for all the home games and Jack Bennett did all the sideline interviews with him. He's a good friend of the station's," I popped. Ha! I got him.

"Well if you know him so well, and he's such a good friend of the station's, why is he not doing your event? I heard you had to cancel."

"No we did not cancel. We are doing something else with the Children's Museum. And what that is—is none of your business."

Okay, where the hell is that shovel? I will beat this jerk to smithereens! My mind was seething.

"Oh Abby, look at the time. Rhonda will be looking for us. We better head on to the Strip." Annie jumped in. She pulled at my arm and headed me off in the other direction. "Bye Greg."

Annie pulled out her phone and called Rhonda, our older sister.

"Girl where are you, Abby is fixin' to have a hissy and I need back-up. Good we'll be down there in a jiff. Rhonda's down at Newks with Vivi and Blake. Let's go. I know they'll help us make a plan. She told me yesterday she was meeting the girls for lunch but I told her we might go to the radio event to spy. But I think it's better now if we just get some food in you before you explode over Greg Galloway.

We walked at a clip down the broken sidewalk past Reese Phifer Hall, where I saw Ben the day before, past the towering shade trees, and on down past Bryant-Denny Stadium. The majestic place just became the number one sports venue in the state, holding well over one hundred thousand. It was a reminder of how lucky we all were to live here. We picked up the pace along the street in front of all the plantation-styled fraternity houses, and all the southern-style mansions. We finally arrived at Newks Cafe. The girls were at a back table and waved us over. Light lunch fare and some of the best salads in Tuscaloosa. Yep I was hungry. Anger makes me that way. I probably needed some Waffle House and then some drinks at The Houndstooth, heavy greasy food and alcohol actually sounded even better. But salads wouldn't make me throw up.

"Hey ladies, come on back here and join us. We've got the bar tab open," Vivi laughed. But one look at Rhonda and she knew me well enough to know I was holding things in, which was my usual way.

"Have a seat here sugar and tell us what's going on," Blake said as she patted the seat between her and Rhonda. I sat down as Rhonda draped her arm around my shoulder.

"I hardly ever see you like this, and like *this*," she said touching my Lilly Pulitzer sweater. What's wrong with you?"

I told the girls what Greg had done and where we had just been. They were all on board now, all of them mad as wet hens.

"Abby, weren't you involved with him a while back?"

Thanks Vivi.

"She was, a couple of times I think. Maybe even recently right honey?"

And thank you Annie. The two biggest mouths of the south began to talk about my past love affairs with Greg. The thing was no one knew why this had made me so mad, I mean on the surface it looked one way but underneath I knew I was at fault. It had been at least a year since Greg had stolen an idea. I was so stupid to let him in again. It *was* me, all my fault. I ran into him about three months ago and he was so smooth. He told me to trust him. Why didn't I listen to my gut? I mean I didn't really even say anything. He did most of the talking, which was par for Greg. His personality precedes him. It was a short tete-a-tete, just an evening—well a night together. It was still winter and I had been out at Five Bar with Annie and Rhonda. Just us sisters on a Friday night. They hugged me bye and I was walking to my car when Greg spotted me and waved. I really didn't want to see him. I have been burned a couple of times by his spying. I mean I can never prove it but I know the promotions are too much alike to be coincidence. So here he comes that night, sauntering over with a grin on his face.

"Hey sweetheart, how's it going these days?" he said dripping with naughtiness. Greg was a big man, tall with dimples, gorgeous dark brown eyes and a thick head of dark brown hair. He had on a long black overcoat and a dark crimson sweater. He always looked sexy, no matter what he wore. It was that flirtatious personality and confident swagger.

His big build was delicious. It could make a girl feel safe. I had only swigged down a couple of mimosas, well, three if we're counting.

"Hey you," I yelled back as Greg crossed the street. *Here we go*, I thought. But I vowed to be strong and not let him too close to me. Uh huh.

"Com'ere you and give me a hug," he blurted. Too late on that not too close idea. I walked across the street, my heels clicking on the pavement. My heart was pounding. The thing about Greg is that he is just purely hard to deny. Even if you say you can't stand him, he's so utterly charming and good-looking that no matter what you feel, you think maybe this time he will be genuine. Somehow you just want his attention. Greg had that ability to make you feel like the only woman he cared about, the only girl in the room. So before I knew it I was in his bear hug, smothered in his embrace and breathing in his delicious cologne. Oh, and I totally forgot how much he irritates me—all within two seconds.

"Don't you look good enough to eat?" He sizzled. "How's it going?"

"You too, great, it's all just great," I managed, still in his arms.

"How long has it been, Abby? Nearly a year since I've even seen you, right?"

"Yeah I think so," I said stepping back. Greg was six feet three and had the cutest baby face I had ever seen, and still all that same thick hair he had in college. I tried to find those feelings of frustration but one look at those dimples and I only felt attraction. Greg was never mean, never a self-aggrandizing narcissist. No, he was fun and funny and so out-going. And all that confidence was just mesmerizing.

"It was last years Alabama Broadcasters Convention down in Mobile. That was one really great time," Greg grinned and winked at me. He was so obviously recalling our reconnection at that event. As I stood there on that cold January night, I stared at him, his words becoming a muffled murmur in the background. Whenever I was around him, things felt good—for the most part.

"Wanna go grab a drink. It's cold out here and it would be great to catch up," he offered. "How 'bout DePalma's? It's cozy and it's right here."

I smiled at him and with everything in me screaming, *Don't do it!* I did.

Drinks and conversation both flowed with ease. I wanted to believe it was because it was us, and we fit well together, but really it was just Greg's way with everyone. He was a charmer. Before I could stop myself, I was in his expensive condo, then in his bed.

I didn't stay all night. I had him drive me back to my car. It was raining a cold sleeting rain. It would have been so much easier just to stay in bed snuggled up to his muscled big body, in those big delicious arms but all I could think of was that I was so weak; either weak or a slutty little fool or both and really I was just so ashamed of myself. See why I said my relationship with Greg was a love hate thing? I am either falling for him, or hating him. This time, which would it be? I knew one thing. Greg Galloway had me. I either wanted to make love to him all night, or beat him with a gardening tool. Not a good match by anyone's standards.

CHAPTER SIX

Today when I saw Greg out there on the quad it was different. I felt like I could actually punch him in the throat. I knew he had to have a spy at my radio station this time, since we had both gone after the Alabama quarterback to draw a crowd. Still he was as gorgeous as ever and that confident swagger almost made me smile—almost.

"Honey, now you know you can't let that man get to you the way he does. He's a player. Just out-play him, that's all," Rhonda offered. "We'll all help if you need us."

"Yes, I'm always in for a good competition," Vivi popped. "And remember, I'm married to the owner of the biggest sports network in Alabama. I've got pull sugar!" And she did. Vivi was married to former Bama wide receiver, Lewis Heart. Everyone in town loved him. But I never wanted to lean on him to help me do my job as promotions director. I wanted to prove myself all on my own.

"Lord, honey, you have sure made the rounds with Greg Galloway, love, hate, love, hate. I'm not sure you'll ever untangle yourself from that man. And you know what they say?" Vivi leaned over as if about to reveal a big secret.

"No, actually I don't. What *do* they say?" I seriously didn't care.

"All that man has to do is crook his finger, and you're right back in his bed."

"And?" Annie spoke up on my behalf.

"And if you can't let him go, you never do."

I sat there thinking. Then—

"Of course I can let him go," I argued. I had, I mean I have, of course I have."

I looked at Annie with a *help me please* look.

Mistake.

"Well, I have news for you, Abby ran into Ben Flannigan yesterday and he has offered to help her too. He even sat with her while she was so upset over all this Greg malarkey....in her car. Just the two of them." Annie sat back in her chair proudly with a smile.

Oh my word, she surely did not just say that. I wanted to poke myself in the eyeballs with my salad fork. I loved this group of ladies, don't get me wrong, but they love to ...let's just say *get involved* in each other's dramas. And right that minute my drama with these two men was fair game for all of them.

Blake could see I was squirming as I took off my Lilly Pulitzer sweater and heaved in a breath like I was fixin' to blow the last little pig's house down. I had gotten suddenly warm and I could feel the heat in my cheeks.

"So I do love the name you picked for Book Club last night. I missed it but Dixie called with the report this morning. Suits you I'd say," Blake nodded and tossed it to me.

"Oh, yes, Zelda. She's my new hero."

"Didn't she wind up in an insane asylum?" Vivi snorted.

"Okay well, you got me there." I shoved a giant forkful of lettuce into my mouth.

Blake shook her head. "That Dixie is a mess? She was just full of it when she called. She actually suggested we start reading the celebrity tabloids for Book Club. Honey, I nearly died.

"It might actually be better than all this Yong Adult style

angst her sister Doreen has been suggesting. All that *"Oh, if I make out with a vampire I might turn into one"* crap has no relation to my life whatsoever."

"Well I can actually relate to neck suckin' more than I can relate to Kim Kardashian's ass. God, if I had that ass I'd have it x-rayed for tumors," Vivi threw her head back and laughed.

"Either that or two ferrets have moved in under her pants," Rhonda popped.

Everyone at the table was laughing. It was just what I needed. I sure did feel so much better.

"Hey Abby, look at it this way. You've got two men who would have you at any moment. I'd say that's pretty good odds. It's really all up to you," Blake reasoned.

Why did I feel like I was missing out? Blake and Vivi both have young children and the two of them aren't much older than me. Rhonda is planning a Christmas wedding to Jack Bennett, Annie has just moved in with Matt Brubaker the studly mountain climber, and then there's me. Mid thirties and single and my biological clock is ticking. *No, you dear Abby are nowhere near having any babies,* I thought to myself. That clock of yours is like a stopwatch wrapped in bubble wrap, swaddled in cotton and shoved into a pickle jar and thrown into the river. I wanted to run away. I could drown my sorrows in a Mountain Dew mimosa and puke my way all the way across the Florida line. How could this be me? How could I be the only one here without any foreseeable future? My future is about as secure as a Pixie Stick during Fashion Week in Manhattan. Change was most definitely overdo.

Lunch ended with hugs and promises to help me get that Greg Galloway once and for all. But did that mean that I would finally stick it to Greg, or he would forever stick it to me—get your mind out of the gutter, you know what I meant.

Annie and I walked back up University Boulevard and back to the Quad on campus. The little carnival was wrapping up. Kids were still in those jumpy houses and the Ferris wheel was unloading the last of the riders. Just then Annie stopped in her tracks.

"Oh my Lord, do you see what I see?"

"What? Greg talking to a blonde? That is certainly nothing unusual."

"Abby, that's not just any blonde, that's Colleen Cantrell, you know, that bimbo Ben dated after you left him. He was with her for like two or three years."

"Is she working for Greg these days?" I asked.

"Looks like it, she's certainly not the type to volunteer labor," Annie surmised. "Wait, her twin sister Cate just applied for a job at our station. I saw her filling out an application last week. She had been filling in downstairs with digital. Abby, she's applying to be your assistant PR director."

I suddenly remembered them from Phi Mu. They were what we called double trouble in the sorority house. They were identical twins, unlike Annie and me. They switched places with each other all the time, especially with men they dated. Now it all makes sense. Colleen and Cate were helping Greg. It had to be. Double Trouble was back to spy on me. But why? I turned to Annie.

"With Cate filling in she must have gotten wind of the PR plans. She must have told Colleen and they beat me to it. Why would Colleen have a problem with me?"

"You have to be an idiot not to see why Colleen would be on board to make you look like you're one step behind," Annie said raising her eyebrow.

"Okay, I'll play. I'm an idiot."

"She was with Ben for years. I bet he pined away for you and that's why he finally had to break it off with her. He never got over you. She's the one out to get you, not Greg."

So that's the way she wants to play? I suddenly knew exactly what I had to do. And I had no time to waste.

CHAPTER SEVEN

Monday morning came quickly. I felt like I finally had a plan to end this little competitive dance with Greg once and for all. The bonus was pretty sweet too. Outsmarting Colleen was just going to be the icing on the cake. Just as I was pulling into work, my cell phone rang in my black leather Michael Kors bag. It was Ben. I felt a smile slide across my face.

"Hey Abby, how was your weekend?"

His deep voice grabbed me off-guard and I suddenly felt like I had a secret weapon against Greg. Ben wouldn't be happy to know that his ex Colleen was working with someone he totally detested. That would make him even more determined to help me put Greg in his place.

"It was fine," I answered. "I went out to the Quad this weekend to do a little spying. Greg threw that promotion we were talking about. I had to see it for myself."

"Ever the curious one, so tell me, what all did you see?" Ben sounded like a port in the storm. But then again, he was playing the part he had always played. I knew I had to be sensitive. He and Colleen had been together a pretty long time. I decided I didn't want to just throw her name out there, so I chose to wait until we had a minute face-to- face.

"Oh, I saw more than I had planned on seeing," I

answered.

"Well go ahead, tell me."

"No, I have an idea. Why don't we meet up later and tell our weekend stories, huh?"

"Sounds like a plan. I had a pretty interesting weekend myself," he alluded.

"Oh really? I can't wait to hear all about it," I said slamming my car door. "Name the place and I'll be there."

"How 'bout Surin on the strip. I can be there by 6. Sound good?"

"Perfect. I love that place. See you then."

"Can't wait," Ben said. "Can I pick you up?"

I thought about that for a minute. That would mean I wouldn't have my car. And, most importantly, it would be more like a date. I wanted to say yes, I mean what's so bad about it being a date? "Uhm…"

"It's not a trick question," Ben laughed. "The parking is just tough in that area so I thought it would be easier to just have one car."

I hesitated only for a second. "Okay sure," I smiled. "Pick me up at 5:30 if that works for you."

"See you then," he said and hung up.

I smiled to myself as I stepped inside the front lobby of the radio station—and my mouth dropped open.

"Hey Abby, remember me? I'm Cate Cantrell."

I nearly swallowed my tongue. I felt like I suddenly had hands squeezing my throat. What was she doing here? I certainly hadn't hired her!

"Uhm, yes, of course, Phi Mu, many years ago as I recall. How can I help you?" I decided to play dumb.

"I am here to begin filling in as your new assistant PR director. I was told there are several final candidates and we will all take a week as kind of a little try-out. I guess I must be first." She chirped. Her smile was wide enough to reveal perfect over-whitened Chiclets for teeth.

"Yes, well please take a seat here in the lobby and I will

send for you in just a few minutes." I backed away and looked at Caroline, the young receptionist. She raised her eyebrows as if to say, *beats me with a stick. I have no idea.* She didn't. But I knew who did; the new station manager. Lewis, Vivi's husband, was the overall General Manager but he was away half the year calling the Alabama football games as their play-by-play announcer. Just under him was Toni Lyn Tingle. And I was headed straight to her office.

"Hey Hon, I have some big news for you," Toni Lyn blurted the minute I flung open her office door. She was smacking her gum, mouth open, as usual and had a nail file in her hand.

"Yes I met her a second ago," I popped. "It would certainly have been nice if someone had informed me first." I slammed her door and stood there in front of her desk, arms folded over my navy jacket. My high-heeled pumps a perfect 8 inches apart, planted firmly on the tapestry carpet.

"Well, someone decided to leave early on Friday or maybe *someone* would have known," she smirked, her giant head of bleached blonde hair perched perfectly still like a white mushroom on her shoulders.

"I do have this new technology called a cell phone. Ever heard of that?"

Toni Lyn stood up and pushed back from behind her perfectly arranged desk

"Now don't getcher panties in a wad, honey. You'll have the final say. I just gotcha started. Now then, Miss Cantrell will be here the first week and then we'll see what we do next. It's all set so get down there and git'r all settled, alrighty?"

Toni Lyn was just poor white trash in anybody's book. She was dressed in solid white from head to toe and it wasn't even past Memorial Day yet. A strict Southern Rule! She looked like she had been melted and poured into her completely out-of-style ensemble. I could see myself like a mirrored reflection in her oversized plumped up lips that were slathered in frosted lipstick that had gone out two decades ago. I shook my head and turned at a clip heading back to the lobby.

I took a dip into the bathroom along the mahogany walled hallway of the old mansion and shut the door behind me. I knew what I had to do and suddenly it hit me that I might just be able to use my new assistant to my benefit. I had to think. I flicked on the light, an antique sconce original to the house, it casting a pinkish glow around the tiny space. The blush pink walls and the tiny hexagon tiles became a cradle for me in that moment. I was totally alone with my thoughts.

I stood there in the silence and looked at myself in the mirror. The muffled sounds of a busy radio station seeped in from underneath the doorway. In a flash I knew I needed a change. Not just my wardrobe, not just my last name with a marriage. I felt an overwhelming sense of uncertainty. What am I building? I was on top of my game, at the top of the ladder; I had gone as far as I could go here. I stared at myself in the amber light of the little powder room and drew in a deep breath. I began to devise a plan. I would use Cate, and if necessary, sweet-talk my way into Greg's little circle. If we were close again, he'd never suspect me of anything. The plan would help us outsmart him on Mother's Day. But then the big announcement would come—I knew I needed to move on. Maybe even do something else with my life.

One more minute of Book Club with Dixie, one more nasty note from my narcissist neighbor Mitzy, and I felt I would come completely undone. I needed to break the routine, and shake things up—put on a neon pink scarf, put the top down and drive outta town. It was time. One last hurrah against the over-confident buffoon Greg and I would quit on top. I looked at myself and nodded as I schemed and dreamed. *Come on, Zelda—we gotta show to put on.* I flicked off the antique light and left the safety of my little pink cocoon.

CHAPTER EIGHT

"My Lord, honey, where's the fire?" Annie said as I ran straight into her in the hallway.

"I am in fire *prevention* mode at the moment. Guess who's waiting in the lobby? None other than one of the evil twins."

"Oh Abby, I saw her. I was comin' to tell you Cate was here. How in hell did that happen?"

"Seems Toni Lyn set up a little audition week and guess who's first at bat?" I smirked and shook my head.

"That Toni Lyn hasn't a brain cell alive in her entire head. Her boobs are up so high in that push up Playtex they're literally cutting off her oxygen."

"Don't worry, I have a plan. A plan for everything I need. It's all worked out in my head."

"Why am I not surprised? Of course you do. You always were the planner." Annie smiled. "I'm glad to see you have it all together. I thought this might throw you for a loop but you seem like your calm old self. Good luck. I'm on the air in five minutes. Oh are you planning to see Mr. Tall Dark and Handsome anymore?"

"He's picking me up after work."

"Oh, I see—*that's* why you're so calm. He always did have that effect on you."

"Uh huh—have a good show," I sassed with one eyebrow up. That was the way she always referred to Ben—tall, dark, and handsome.

"And remember you have to tell me the big bad plan okay?" Annie popped.

"Go! You're gonna miss your cue."

Abby slipped into her studio across from the powder room and the red 'on air' light popped on. She was great at what she did. She could always match-make and now she was getting paid to help people find their lost loves. She was the one who put our sister Rhonda with our Sports host, Jack Bennett. Jack and Rhonda had met at summer camp when they were in their early teens. It was so romantic the way she helped them find each other. He had already proposed. All they needed to do was set the date. I seemed to be the soon- to- be- old maid in the house. It was my childhood dream come true. Old maid. Maybe I was just way too picky. I mean if Toni Lyn-white-trash could get a man, what the hell was my problem? Maniac Mitzy was married to an accountant. I hate Maniac Mitzy. Her husband stays always gone away on business. Of course he does. He hates her too.

Suddenly, "God, Cate, you have to be careful in this hallway, dear." As I turned to continue on to my doom, er, destiny with Cate, she ran smack-dab into my chest. *It's okay honey, I have another boob. I didn't need that one,'* I thought to myself. *And we know everybody loves a uni-boob.*

"Ohmygoodness, I am so sorry, Abby. I had no idea you were right there," Miss Phi Mu oozed.

"No problem. I'll live," I smiled. "Okay ready?" I chirped excitedly. It was an act. "We have so much to do. C'mon. I'll get you started." I knew if I was gonna make this plan work I had to get her to like me. The thing was, we were never that close during college. She was always trying to help her twin sister get to Ben. And that usually meant trying to undermine me. Colleen always had a thing for Ben, so when I was finally out of her way, she wound up with him. But now I had to act like all of that was in the past—you know, like an adult. I led her to my office, and then showed her to her desk, just outside in the upstairs foyer. I had to play it all very close. I wanted to mention that I knew her sister was working for Greg but I knew I had to keep that to myself for now. If she thought I might suspect something she would be much less open with me, much less free with her words and actions. I wanted her to think I was in the dark. I decided to always keep my door open. I wanted to be able to see her at all times, and most importantly hear her. I could even see if she was texting.

Also, the most important thing—by the end of the week I would tell Toni Lyn that we need not see anyone else for the assistant PR director position. I would hire her outright and by the time we got to the big Mother's Day event, it would be revealed—how she was helping her sister by spying on the station and me. Hopefully I could pull this off then ride off into the sunset. I didn't want to seem pushy and blow my cover so I was very slow, very accommodating. By the end of the day, she was in the palm of my hand. I saw her texting a couple of times but for that first day I was silent and just let her get all comfy out there at her desk.

Annie came darting up after her show and in typical Annie fashion nearly spilled the beans.

"Alrighty honey, I'm waiting. Tell me everything!" She slammed my door and plopped on my red toile printed sofa just across from my desk.

"Have you totally lost your mind?" I said through clenched teeth. "Cate is sitting right there."

"Oh was I rude?" Annie jumped up and opened the door. "Hey Cate, I didn't even see you sitting there sugar," Annie said to Cate. "How's the first day goin'?"

I suddenly could not believe I was surrounded by so many blondes.

Annie shut the door once again and settled back onto the couch.

"I know you aren't really that dumb blonde you pretend to

be," I sassed.

"Silly, of course not. I knew you had secrets to spill, you know, the big plan and all, so I smartly closed the door so she couldn't hear us. Since you know, we are planning against her—sorta," she explained.

"I retract my last statement, judge. Let the last statement of my sister stand as proof of the dumb blonde identity."

"Huh?" Annie asked with her head cocked to one side.

"Oh Annie, I have to keep an eye on her at all times," I explained. "I can't talk here, she could hear us. I will call you later tonight and clue you in okay? Just open the door. She could be calling her sister."

"Oh poo. I wanted to know the plans. I was all excited." Annie got up and opened the door and stuck her head out, "Sorry sugar. No reason to shut the door. Just habit."

I looked at my sister and just shook my head. "Okay," Annie continued, "Just remember you have to call me tonight. Matt is coming home tomorrow and I have a big Welcome Home surprise for him, so I may be tied up. Literally."

"I'll bet."

"Well you have a date with Ben tonight, right?"

"Yes, but really it's not a *date*. Just a quick bite to eat and some planning."

Annie was now shaking her head at me.

"You are so clueless," she reasoned. "You don't understand men whatsoever do you? I think that has always been your problem."

"Okay, first of all, there are so many things about that statement that make me wonder. I am not clueless, I am careful, and what do you mean, *that has always been my problem*? I don't *have* a problem, especially with men."

"Sweetheart, you live in a bubble. A bubble of dark suits, no ring and no man. You clearly have no clue about men and what they want. That is not even debatable."

"I'll beg your pardon, I have certainly had my share of men!"

"Oh really? Who? Ben and Greg. Then Greg and Ben then Greg and now Ben. That, sugar, is certainly *not plenty*. That is two. Two. Even I can do that math."

I sat there. She had me. Two. That was it. My whole life. Just the two of them. Oh I had a date here and there but none that lasted past a single night out. I had both Greg and Ben as a lover. That is all of my information regarding sex and men. My experience with the male species would fit on a post-it note. By that definition alone, I *was* actually clueless.

But not Annie. She was the resident Marilyn Monroe. Sultry, sexy and curves in all the most perfect places, she oozed femininity. I was the bookish brunette. Fraternal twins, she got the curves and I got the small frame and flat stomach...and lack of curves. I did have long gorgeous hair and she and I did share my mother's fabulous blue eyes. Annie had a whispery sexy voice too, and those poor lovelorn show listeners just loved her. She was a southern belle to her core. Sometimes I thought we were destined to be like those Steel Magnolia characters. I was certain that if things kept going the way they had been, she would surely become *Clairee* and I was pretty positive I was headed straight to becoming *Weezer*. Delightful.

CHAPTER NINE

It was nearly 5:30 and Ben would be arriving to pick me up soon. I slipped into the little pink powder room again to touch up my make-up. I added mascara, and slid on my perfect pale pink lipstick. I touched up my face powder and added a pop of blush. As I zipped my red leather make-up bag closed I glanced up at myself in the mirror. I suddenly began to feel my heart quicken. I was nervous. Annie was right. This was a date, no matter how you sliced it. I knew I still cared so much for Ben. Suddenly my phone rang sending a jolt through my stomach.

"Hey Abby, I'm out here," Ben informed. "I just wanted to let you know in case you weren't quite ready. No hurry. We have plenty of time."

"Nope, I'm done. I'll be right out." I hung up and took one last look in the mirror. Did I *want* this to be a date? I blew out a breath to ease my nerves. The answer was yes. Yes, I did want this to be a date. The question was, did Ben?

I opened the huge antique mahogany door. It was another fixture original to the house and had survived the restoration that transformed the majestic home into the radio station. Lewis was amazing and went to a ton of trouble to save the old place. He restored it and turned it into WRCT. The wide front porch was so fragrant with azaleas and wisteria dripping from hanging baskets dangling from the wooden ceiling. A breeze hit me just as I turned to head down the front staircase. The Deep South was the most fragrant place on earth in the springtime.

Ben sat in his little red vintage roadster. He looked adorable. I made my way over to his car and as I walked he got out. I suddenly remembered that Ben was such an old-fashioned gentleman. I also recalled just how much I loved that.

"Hey, you! How was your day?" He greeted me with a quick but tight hug. It felt good.

"It was an adventure. I'll tell you all about it," I smiled as he walked around the car with me and opened my door. I slid onto the tanned leather seats. This car was most definitely vintage. It was perfect for Ben. His tall frame and dark hair made him look like he was right out of Downton Abby sitting in this old delicious relic.

"I love this car. What kind is it?" I began the conversation.

"Isn't it great? He grinned. "It was actually my dad's car. It's a vintage Triumph TR3, 1958. He kept it in such great condition. Purrs like a kitten and hugs the road. I love it." He was obviously very proud of it. But he would be, mostly because it was his dad's. Ben was the most family-centric guy I had ever met. He was like that in college too. I had never known a guy that would take his parents' calls at any time. And he always ended the conversations with an, *I love you.* He had told me all about his family. He was the oldest of two. He had a younger sister who was now a veterinarian. She was the family vet for their horse farm up in north Alabama. Equine medicine was her specialty. It was a family business and it was actually pretty nice to see a family so tightly knit. It was certainly part of what made Ben who he was.

"Well, it certainly suits you," I bubbled.

We sped out of the front lot of the radio station, the evening sun shining as we headed to campus. Conversation ebbed as we took off, the wind rushing through my hair along Hargrove Road, across 15th street and left onto University Boulevard. Ben glanced over and smiled as he shifted gears. I felt like a 1940s movie star. Next time, I promised myself, I would wear a scarf on my head and tie it under my chin like Audrey Hepburn. This certainly took me out of my routine, the predictable life I had created for myself. Safe. It was what I thought I had wanted, until I ran into Ben last Friday.

He pulled his car right to the curb just down from the restaurant.

I sat still and fumbled in my purse, quickly grabbed my compact and checked myself as Ben walked around and opened my door. This would take some getting used to. I suddenly stopped myself. I was acting like Ben and I were getting back together and he had shown me no sign of that whatsoever. I reminded myself, this is just dinner. *Don't get ahead of yourself Abby. And surely don't come across as desperate.*

"Are you hungry?" Ben asked as I stepped out, my black patent pumps touching the pavement. The cool of the evening was just ahead and the soft perfumed air relaxed me as I stood up from the car. Ben reached around me to close the door. He was close enough that I could smell his aftershave. I hadn't been that close to a man in so long. After my little one night fling with Greg at the Broadcasters Convention, I had sworn off men for a while. Well, I surely hadn't planned on it being *this* long but I kinda just poured myself into my work. It seemed that no matter what, I couldn't help myself when it came to Greg. He was dangerous for me. I knew he could never love me as much as he loved himself and his job. He could be infuriating and anytime I had been with him, no matter what, in the end, all I felt was lonely and like the bottom wrung of his ladder. Ben never ever left me feeling like anything but his total priority. How could I have been so stupid? And just how is it that a guy like Ben is still available?

We walked next to each other down the sidewalk and

slipped into Surin. It was a scrumptious Thai place on the famous Strip just down University Boulevard from the stadium. It was warm and friendly, very casual and the aromas literally leapt to the sidewalk and dragged you in if you were just passing by. Although the place was homey, every table boasted white table clothes and cotton fabric napkins. Ben met the hostess and gave his name and she showed us to a little table for two in the back. Amber lighting lit the space and cast a warm light on Ben's sweet face as he pulled out my chair at the little table.

"Thanks," I whispered. Ben just smiled as he sat down across from me.

The waitress handed us menus and took our drink orders. Ben ordered a Chardonnay. "Are you still drinking white these days?" He asked me.

I nodded.

"Make that two of those," he finished.

The waitress smiled and walked away. Ben looked across at me, his blue eyes twinkling and spoke.

"So tell me all about your weekend," he began. "It sounded pretty interesting if you went out to see Greg's big event."

"Well it was. Greg was so nice, like he had no idea. He actually said I could come over and meet the quarterback. I was like, uhm, I kinda know him since I have promoted him being on with Jack before. He was typical Greg."

I hesitated to tell him about Colleen but I wanted to see his reaction. I also wanted to be as sensitive as I could without putting him in an awkward position. I continued.

"Anyway we didn't talk to him but just a second."

"We?" he looked up at me.

"Oh yeah, me and Annie. She was the one who talked me into going. She wanted to see just what they had planned."

"Oh," Ben smiled as if he was wondering if I had gone with a man. I hoped that was what he was wondering anyway.

We met up with Blake and Vivi, and Rhonda had some

lunch, talked and then Annie and I headed back to the Quad. The event was all but over. Pretty boring until we saw who the new assistant PR director was."

"Oh yeah, who?"

"It was Colleen. Colleen Cantrell." There it was. It was out there. Ben stopped smiling and smirked.

"Well good for her. She was pretty good at PR. Not like you were but then she is just his assistant. I really haven't seen her in over a year."

"I just know she and her sister are up to something," I pitched.

"Cate? What does Cate have to do with anything? Don't tell me she's working with Greg too," Ben pushed.

"Nope, she's working for me as of today." I popped up my eyebrows and shook my head.

"Okay, Okay, back up a minute. How did that happen on the heels of just seeing Colleen?"

I explained the logistics as the waitress delivered our wine, setting the flutes down gently on the white tablecloth. She took our orders, chicken in peanut sauce for me and curry shrimp for Ben. The waitress left and I finished the long explanation of how Toni Lyn had set up this ridiculous audition process and just what I planned to do.

"So, I was thinking this is where you could maybe help me with that intern idea. Are you still thinking you could do that? I mean I surely don't want to put you in an awkward position."

"Sure, I need to talk to one of my teaching assistants. I will do it in the morning and let you know."

"The plan is to give Cate the job and watch her as closely as we can. I think she will give it away before she realizes what she's doing. Plus she's right outside my office and I can hear her perfectly. There is no way she and her sister aren't up to something with them both working at competing stations and for competing bosses."

Ben seemed suddenly defensive. "I never knew Colleen to be like that. And I certainly never knew her to be a big fan of

Greg Galloway."

I wasn't sure how to take this information and his defense of her. I also knew there was no way I would tell him the core of my plan. To get close enough to Greg to make him slip. Ben wouldn't trust me. And things were already off to the perfect evening. The thing was, I was a tad worried myself about getting too close to Greg. He knew I was weak where he was concerned but this time it would be different. I promised myself.

CHAPTER TEN

The evening light outside was slowly fading and I watched as each streetlight shimmered on just steps from the huge front windows of the little restaurant. I decided things were getting too heavy and the conversation was becoming tense. Ben seemed uncomfortable and I wasn't ready to end the night. I changed the subject.

"So tell me all about your weekend," I urged.

Ben relaxed and leaned back in his chair. "Well it was pretty good. Memorable I'd say. We may have a horse in the Derby this year."

"Oh Ben, that is wonderful! Tell me everything!"

"We have a fast little filly and I think she is hitting her prime at the perfect time. We have just enough time to get her credentials and paperwork. She's won enough pre-lims so we think this may be her year."

"Oh that is so thrilling. I never knew your family kept any of the horses. I thought they just bred and sold them."

"Well we had to keep this one. She was a runt and her mother rejected her, so I took over. It was nearly summer three years ago and school had just let out so I went home and helped out. I nursed her and she just kinda became ours. We didn't want to sell her." I could tell Ben was so proud, his blue eyes glistening in the candlelight.

"I can't believe I may know one of the horses," I beamed. "You know we never miss the Derby. We make a day of it, all of us girls in our big hats and we make mint juleps and watch the pre-shows and everything! I'm so excited for you. For your whole family."

Ben looked at me. He was grinning.

"What? Do I have something on my face?" I asked brushing my cheeks with my hands.

"No. You're just so damn cute. You always were," he smiled. Ben lowered his eyes and leaned forward. My fingers slid up and down the long stem of my glass. I glanced up as my eyes met Ben's. I felt a flush rise and my cheeks became hot. Ben brushed his fingers against my skin, pushing his glass closer to mine. He looked like he was about to tell me a secret.

"I have an idea," he teased. "Wanna see it in person this year?" He asked with a twinkle in his bright blue eyes.

"My heart skipped and I felt a shiver slide down my spine. "Oh Ben! Oh my gosh! Yes! Are you kidding me? Yes yes, of course I do! When is it?"

"You know, the first Saturday in May. The 7th I think."

"Oh no! I have a huge event planned for Mother's Day. I've already reserved the venue. Oh no," I sighed. "I can't pass up the chance to see the Derby with you. I can't believe this!"

"Abby, look at me. We will figure it all out. We will. The Derby is on Saturday. We can get back here for the event on Sunday. It will work out," Ben promised. He smiled a sincere smile. He was so genuine. "You seem so jittery," he continued. "I know you're going through a lot right now at work but you were always so calm and centered."

"I know it, it's just that all this competition is finally getting to me. I have this plan and to be honest, I'm not totally sure I can pull it off. I know Greg's station is planning something for Mother's Day too and their venue is just across the street from ours."

Ben laughed and folded his arms. "Now that is just

brilliant. I seriously cannot wait for that." He leaned back and folded his arms, shaking his head.

The waitress brought the food and re-filled our wine glasses. Dinner was so savory and sweet. We chatted some more, mostly small talk. And then the past came up. And yes, I was the idiot who brought it up. I must be allergic to Chardonnay. Booze always makes me say things I regret.

"Ben, I need to tell you something," I began innocently enough. "I'm really sorry about the way things ended with us. I was just young and really stupid." *Kinda like right now*, I thought to myself. *Okay well not so young—just stupid.*

"Abby seriously we don't have to talk about it. We're friends now. It's all fine." Ben squirmed in his chair. "I'm really glad I ran into you last week. It's been way too long."

I took a breath and tried to relax. Me and relax aren't usually used in the same sentence, ever. I like my carefully made plans and I like to execute those plans in perfect order. That is what relaxes me—not winging it and hoping for the best.

The waitress showed up and I shook my head scaring her away. She bit her lip and backed up.

"No, Ben it isn't really over. It never has been. I was just not ready back then and I feel so badly about everything. I have for such a long time." *I just had to keep talking.*

"I promise you. No hard feelings. I really am fine, and look at you, you are too. Right?" Ben was trying to diffuse the situation.

I had to bite my own lip to stop myself from answering him. The truth was I still had feelings for Ben. So no, I wasn't totally fine. I smiled and took a sip of wine and leaned back in my chair. My mouth wanted to keep going but I couldn't move it with my teeth biting into my lip. I gazed at Ben. He was holding in a laugh, I could tell.

"What? Are you fixin' to laugh at me?"

"No. I swear I wouldn't laugh at you. But, seriously you are still the cutest girl I ever knew," he said as he pursed his lips together then reached across the table and grabbed my hand. "Come on," he pulled, "I have a little surprise for you." He left cash on the table and slid his chair back and before I could focus my wine infused eyes, we were outside on the sidewalk. Students buzzed around, up and down the strip, ducking into bars and shops. The twilight skies were deep blue and the amber streetlights warmed the little corner of the sidewalk.

"Where are you taking me?" I asked him as he pulled me behind him.

Ben was suddenly giddy as he ran up the street to his little roadster, holding my hand the entire way. He opened my door and I slid in. He closed the door in a hurry and ran around the back, jumping in over the side of the car to get into the driver's seat. The engine revved, Ben shifted the gears and we were off. Where, I didn't know. But I didn't care. I felt such freedom in that moment—more than I had felt in more years than I could count. I couldn't control this situation. I couldn't plan and worry. I didn't need to make a list. I was just along for the ride, the open top, the darkening skies, the warm spring night air sliding across my bare skin as he drove. He looked over and winked at me. Was I dreaming? Was it possible? Was I about to have the time of my life with the one that got away? A second chance—maybe I should make that the one that *almost* got away.

CHAPTER ELEVEN

Ben drove out to the edge of town. I wanted to reach over and rest my hand on his thigh the way we used to in college. I wanted him to reach for my hand and lace his fingers in mine. But we weren't there yet. Ben and I were not anything but friends getting reacquainted. It was so comfortable with Ben next to me, so familiar. But awkward in that neither of us knew just how to respond to each other.

Ben took the old two-laned blacktop past the cemetery and out past the old Baptist church and curved into an open clearing of grass just beyond the last dirt turn-off. We were completely alone, top down on the vintage Triumph, when Ben rolled to a quiet stop. Ben turned off the engine and then switched off the lights. It was like we had been draped in black velvet with only the faint light of the crescent moon glimmering behind a lone tree branch.

Ben looked at me and smiled the smallest little grin. It was eerily quiet. I could hear his breathing. The silence draping around us and filling in with the darkness. "Look up," he whispered.

I leaned my head back to see a jillion stars glistening like sequins on the navy backdrop of the cloudless night sky. He remembered.

"What do you think?" He whispered.

"I don't think I have ever seen this many stars at one time. I can't believe it. It is so amazing, Ben."

"Abby, I know you always wished on stars. The entire time we were together you would lie back and gaze at the night sky and wish on falling stars, or the first star of the evening. You would have me pull over sometimes so you could make your wishes. I wanted to bring you here tonight so you know, your wishes are still alive—and still important."

I laid my head back on the headrest of my seat and scanned the stars. My favorite, Orion and to the upper right, Pleiades. Orion was brighter than the moon that night. Orion's belt twinkled as a faint smile crept across my satisfied face. This was Ben at his core. Thinking of me and doing for me, and his only thought in this moment was my happiness. His memory of me from all those years ago, though we had both moved on with other people, was as pure as the night sky — genuine and authentic. Ben was soft in his soul. Peaceful. I felt myself relax and my breathing hit a rhythm, steady and quiet. I closed my eyes.

"What is your wish tonight?" Ben murmured, careful not to intrude on the silence that fell around us.

I smiled with my eyes still closed. "You know I can't tell you. I would have to kill you," I teased.

"You never would tell me any of your wishes," Ben recalled. I kept my eyes closed and I could feel the heat of his face near mine. My heart quickened as his breath tickled my ear.

"I always wanted to know what swirled in that beautiful head of yours and you would never tell me," he continued. Remember your nickname?"

"Of course I do," I smiled recalling the moniker. "It was Stardust. Every time I would be looking up at the night sky you would ask me the same thing."

"I know," he interrupted. "Whatcha looking at Stardust? It suited you then and it suits you now."

"I loved it when you called me that. I never told anyone. It was one of those things that was just ours. Like so many moments, and inside jokes.

"I know, Abby. We will always have that you know? It's like those things that only certain couples have. Those nameless shared little things and it only happens when two become one. A look can become an entire conversation. I always thought we had that thing, whatever it is. At least I felt it with you."

I knew exactly what he meant. We did. I could look at him from across a room and he could read my mind. We had so many shared little things. An energy between us, linking us as one, even back then. I had messed it up for us. But I was feeling a new second chance on the horizon. I was nervous but I wanted to give it a shot.

"We did have that thing," I affirmed. "We always did. I kinda think we still do."

I felt Ben move, the heat of his skin on mine sent tingles down my shoulders. Then, I felt him rest his warm lips on my cheek. He took a chance that we could be more that just friends getting reacquainted. I loved that he was so vulnerable yet bold in his decision, willing to see what this kiss might bring.

I kept my eyes closed as a smiled slid across my lips. Another soft kiss on my cheek, as Ben whispered, "Is this okay?"

"Yes," I answered softly.

"How about this?" Ben asked slipping ever closer to my mouth.

"Yes," I said again.

"And how about this?" Ben slurred as he rested his lips on mine, soft and warm, it was the most delicious feeling I had experienced in so long. I felt my skin prickle down the back of my neck as my flesh felt a flush of heat rising inside me. I didn't want to push him and make a fool of myself. Feeling Ben's mouth on mine was wonderful, familiar and safe and exciting all at the same time. He wandered my lips and I let him as long as he wanted to. He kissed me so gently one last time before pulling back. I opened my eyes slowly to see Ben's beautiful face still leaning over mine.

"Abby, I hope that was okay. I mean it's really hard to be near you here under the stars and not remember all we felt for each other."

"Ben, I know. You didn't see me try to pull away. I feel just the same. I remember too—hundreds of nights of sitting under a canopy of stars, wishing and holding hands and kissing and dreaming." I looked at Ben deeply to gauge his reaction. I felt myself wanting him all over again. I felt so safe. I was consumed with a security I maybe never had felt. Ben and I were so young before. But now we were older, in the throws of our careers, more stable and more focused. He was a man, successful and steady. In that moment I felt like he was exactly what I needed.

"We had the world by the tail," he said with a grin. "It was just us and we could do anything we wanted—together," I cooed.

"I know. It was the time of my life, being with you. I never forgot it, but I knew you weren't coming back. I knew you had such big dreams and who was I really to hold you back? I was just content with you—you alone. But you needed so much more. The life in broadcasting was so exciting for you. You know, back then I used to think all those wishes you wished were all for your life in the radio business. You craved it so, Abby. I hope you have been happy. Satisfied. You have certainly been incredibly successful." Ben lifted his hand to my cheek and curled my long dark hair behind my ear and smiled, his blue eyes glistening in the moonlight. "I was always really proud of you."

I drew in a breath and leaned my head back. No matter what I did to him, Ben was still so proud of me. I was in awe of his genuine honesty. But I knew just what he was saying. It was an old conversation. It used to come up as often as the sun. *What would we do after graduation?* I talked incessantly of working in Birmingham then moving on to the larger markets of Atlanta and then with all my tenacity, I would stake my claim in the Big Apple. Ben and I never wanted the same things—at least back then. He was much more settled—that old soul who wanted home and family and weekends at the Gulf. What had I really done? I did go to Birmingham for a few years, then I was off to Atlanta for a year. Ever the list maker, I was checking things off, going according to my big plan. But then it all ended. I was fired in Atlanta after a drop in ratings. Blind-sided, I came home to Tuscaloosa and worked a few odd jobs, mostly doing PR and marketing for retail. Then I found a job back in radio at a small station and slowly began to rebuild my reputation and my life.

All the while I knew Ben was dating Colleen, I stayed clear of them. It was a painful past with things ending the way they did, and honestly I was embarrassed. I had left him nearly at the alter, not totally because we were so young—but mostly because I had such drive—such ambition. I wanted to hit the big-time. But these days, I was so tired and just longed for some peace and easy breathing—just like I was having right that moment, sitting under the stars with Ben. It just felt really right.

"You shouldn't have been so proud of me, Ben. I left you on one knee out at the lake. I was crazy and I'm so so sorry—for all of it." I couldn't say anymore.

Ben put his index finger over my lips and shook his head. He moved closer and pressed his lips to mine. I kissed him back softly. Ben was tender and slow. He pulled back and smiled again. "Never again apologize for being true to you heart, Abby. I always admired you for that."

I looked up at the stars again.

"Look, there's Pleiades," Ben pointed. "It was always your favorite."

"How did you remember that?"

"You taught me all about the night sky. I never look at the stars that I don't look for Orion and Pleiades. How could I forget with all the hours we spent lying in the back of my old red truck staring at the dark sky? Those were some of my favorite times, Abby. My favorite memories. We'd take some hot chocolate out and my old plaid flannel blanket and head out to the fields and make a cozy night of it. I remember sometimes you fell asleep in my arms under those stars. They were the very best of times, remember?"

I laid my head on his shoulder and looked up at the twinkling stars in Orion's belt. I closed my eyes and made a wish. One very secret wish. And this time, it had nothing to do with my career or a radio station or a promotional event or even to out-smart Greg. I knew what I wanted, maybe for the first time in my life.

CHAPTER TWELVE

The sunny morning peeked through my bedroom curtains and pulled me out of a sound deep sleep. Was last night a dream? I hadn't felt so much serenity in an eternity. Was this really going somewhere this time? Ben made me feel safe and wanted. I had always lived a day ahead, with all my planning and prepping for events; it just trains the mind that way. But last night stargazing with Ben had me living in the present. Nothing else mattered last night. It was just us. Just like it was so long ago. No pressure. No calendars. It was perfect.

I showered and dressed and flew downstairs in a hurry. I had so much to do that day to get the plan against WRBI rolling in time for the Mother's Day event. I hurried through my toast and coffee and flung the front door open only to find 10 hot pink azaleas along with their root ball all over my front porch. Mitzy! Ugh! She had wanted the gorgeous azaleas removed form the shared alley-way because she is allergic. So here they were, dying all around my front door. And of course she left a nice little note:

Dear Ms. Harper,

Since you have not attended to the problem with the shared alley-way, I had my gardener Roofus remove the allergy-inducing shrubs and return them to you. I asked him to keep the root-ball in case you would like to plant them elsewhere but of course nowhere near my side of your home. Thank you for the wonderful housewarming gift but I cannot tolerate flowers of any kind so it would be appreciated if you could relocate any other flowering bushes to the eastern side of your property. Oh yes, and please take this as it is meant, with all good intentions. Those Hilary Clinton suits you wear age you dreadfully. Ruffled blouses and Dynasty-esque shoulder pads went out eons ago. You might not be so single and lonely if you learned how to dress. If you would like, I am a personal life-coach by trade and I think I could be of great help to you. How about a glass of wine tonight when you get home and we can begin my new Change Your Life Program? I am quite certain you will benefit from my savvy suggestions.

Have a wonderful day!
~Mitzy Montgomery
Life Coach and Personal Developer.

I felt the rage rise till I thought my head would pop off. I made a dramatic pivot and went back inside to write Mitzy Montgomery a wake up call of her own.

Dear Ms. Montgomery,

Thanks so much for the wine invitation this evening but I must respectfully decline. Despite what you think of my pitiful existence as a lonely old maid, I have plans tonight. And they do involve a man. I personally don't believe in life coaches, especially the ones who have no life. As far as my "Clinton-esque" pantsuits, you would have no idea how to dress for a career since you can obviously work in the darkened, flowerless house you call home, similar to Hannibal Lecter. I see you are trying to mimic Pippi Longstocking since you live in your blue jean cutoffs. They are far too snug. I am continually surprised that your chubby thighs don't ignite when you are out sweeping that porch for the tenth time in one day. Seriously, Mitz—it's not a pretty picture.

Regarding your vandalism of the shared alley-way, I

expect you to hire a professional contractor, not some guy named Roofus, to restore the space to pristine condition within the week. When I am satisfied that it has been properly restored, I will return your mailbox.
Sincerely,
Abigail Harper,
AKA, Ms. Pantsuit.

I marched next door and dropped the note on her porch, turned and walked at a clip to the end of her sidewalk, adrenaline rushing, I bear-hugged her mailbox and with one yank released it from the dirt and carried it straight into my house in my high-heeled pumps.

I drove to work with a grin on my face. But it didn't last long once I stepped inside WRCT. I was met in the front hall by Cate, my new assistant.

"Oh Ms. Harper, I've been waitin' on you. All hell's breakin' loose. That event for Mother's Day may have to be rescheduled."

"Cate, in case you can't figure this one out on your own, Mother's day cannot be rescheduled!"

"Well, the Friedman House called you this mornin' and since you weren't here yet, I took the call."

"Fabulous! A+ for you today."

"Anyway, they said there may be a mix-up in the calendar and you will need to call right away."

"No. That house is mine on Mother's Day. I paid them a huge deposit yesterday on the company card."

"I don't know anything more, but just give them a call. Here's the number. Oh Ms. Harper, this has me as nervous as a cat in a room fulla rockin' chairs, honey. We may need another location."

I immediately sensed something was up. And it wasn't just Cate's enormous boobs. She trotted back across the hall and up the curved staircase on the tiptoes of her pointy high heels. Her tousled bleached hair bounced along with her chest as she pranced. Something just smelled funny about this whole situation. I held the sticky-note with the number in my hand as I made my way up the stairs to my office.

As soon as I was behind my desk and comfortable, I called the number.

"Good morning, Battle-Friedman Home. How may I help you?"

I told the woman on the other end that I was returning her call regarding the date of the event.

"Oh yes, Ma'am. It looks like someone had booked us for their wedding shower just a minute before you called and no one had written down your reservation. May I book another date for you instead?"

"Well, nope unless you can convince America to move Mother's Day this year."

"Oh, I see. Well, no need to get snarky with me. I am very sorry but we are booked. Unless there is another date, we cannot be of any further service. Thanks for the call."

Just then Annie came twirling in, her 1950s vintage dress swaying as she walked. This was a typical wardrobe for her. Annie always dressed in vintage 1950s attire. It went right along with her talk show for the love-lost. I looked up and shook my head at her.

"Hey girlie, let me think, bad day and it's only 9:30 in the morning?"

I smirked.

"Either that or your sensible navy pumps are too tight. Which is it?"

"Close the door," I ordered.

"Okay but you told me to never close the door the other day."

"This is an amendment," I pushed. Annie closed the office door and took her place on the over-stuffed couch.

"What's going on?" she asked fluffing her dress in a perfect circle around her.

"Cate took a message this morning and looks like they double-booked the Friedman Home so we can't have it for the

Mother's Day event."

"Oh no! Let me see what I can do. I know the girl that books the place, maybe I can pull some strings."

"I just spoke to her. She called me snarky."

"Jeanette? No, she would never say that. She's so sweet. That doesn't sound at all like her. I think I can handle it. When I get off the air I will run by and see her."

"Oh Annie, that would be awesome. I just think something sounded funny about this whole thing. I'm gonna investigate a little while you're on the air."

"Don't worry, honey. I got this, okay? I gotta run. Showtime's coming up fast." Annie stood up and straightened her dress and blew me a kiss. She opened the door and glanced back at me, rolling her eyes.

"Leave it open," I remarked. Annie winked and turned the corner toward the steps and was out of sight. I looked out at Cate. She was texting. Oh how I wanted to see what she was up to.

"Cate," I called out. "I'm gonna need you to start finding a new location for our event right away."

"Oh, yes ma'am. I'm on it."

I wanted to rip her phone out of her teeny little hands and read it. I wanted to scream, *no texting at work*, but I seriously knew she would hang herself if I gave her enough rope. I had to be patient. I suspected she was texting her sister. Suddenly my own cell phone rang in my bag. I pushed back from desk and stood up, walking over to the credenza under the window and fumbled through until I felt the smooth sides of the device. I answered quickly.

"Hello this is Abby Harper."

"Good morning Abby Harper. How is my stargazer?"

It was Ben. His deep voice was like a sedative.

"Hey you. I'm okay. How are you this morning?"

"Can't stop thinking of last night. I had a really nice time," he oozed.

"Me too, I woke up happy."

"Good, I hope you stay that way all day."

I would, I thought, but I've had a run-in with Ms. Life Coach Thunder Thighs, and then with the Playboy Bunny, the sneak here at work. So far today has been quite a winner. But I didn't want to be all Debbie Downer to Ben.

"I'll try," I promised.

"I wanted to let you know, I talked to my TA this morning. She's young, a first year grad student and I told her what was happening. She agreed to help us out and I have arranged to send her over as a PR intern for Greg and Colleen. Her name is Janie Walsh. She's really smart. Colleen didn't suspect a thing when I called her this morning."

"Oh," I hesitated. Why did it fluster me when Ben mentioned Colleen's name? He and Colleen had been long over and she was certainly no threat. Not that she ever was. Still, I felt a pang in the pit of my stomach. For this plan to work, Ben would have to be in a type of cooperation with Colleen. She would be handling his intern. I had to be okay with it.

"What? Is something wrong?" Ben was in tune to say the least.

"Uhm, no, It's all fine. Promise."

"Why don't we talk about it over lunch?" He proposed.

"Oh Ben, I wish I could. I'm so swamped here today. I'm gonna skip lunch I think. But we can meet for dinner if you aren't busy," I suggested.

"You're on. I'll let you know how it goes for Janie. She's over there meeting everyone today."

"Okay," I agreed. "Call me when you get off today and we can work out the dinner plans," I said. "Can't wait to see you."

"Me, too Abby. Have a good one."

Ben hung up, but I held the phone pressed against my cheek for a few more seconds. He was good—just purely good all the way down to his old soul. I smiled to myself.

"It's not good for you to skip lunch, ya know." Cate hollered from the grand hall outside my door. "It's not healthy."

Oh God, I thought, *did she hear me?* I quickly scrolled back what I had said to Ben. Did I mention her sister's name out loud? Did I say anything that would tip off the bimbo? I cringed.

"Know what else isn't healthy?" I yelled back to her.

"No, what?" She chirped

"Eavesdropping." I hissed.

"Why is that unhealthy?" Miss Bimbo popped.

"It could get you killed." I threatened.

CHAPTER THIRTEEN

Noon came and Annie went on the air. I was stir crazy wondering what was happening with everything. Suddenly so much was going on. Between Ben and his intern, Colleen and Cate and now the venue for my event being changed. And of course now, Ben and me, I suddenly felt like I had hands around my throat. I needed some air. Cate had left minutes ago, so I grabbed my new red leather Kate Spade, dropped my phone inside and headed down the back staircase. The back exit led me past Annie's studio. I waved at her as I headed back through the kitchen and out the door and down the steps. I walked around to the front lot and opened my car door. Sliding in I took a deep breath as my door slammed. It just felt good to be alone and in the quiet solitude of my car.

I called Ben but it went to voicemail. I drove out to the strip, and on into downtown. I pulled into a space near Mellow Mushroom. The delicious smells of garlic and mozzarella dragged me inside. I needed a mimosa but I knew better than to drink mid-day. I walked inside and sat down at a little table for two near the window. Suddenly a tap on the shoulder.

"What's a pretty lady doin' here all by herself?" Oh no, it was Greg. My stomach heaved and dropped all in one move. He was the very last person I needed to see. I wasn't quite ready to enact my plan. The idea that I would let myself get close to him to find out just what I needed to know wasn't really quite developed yet. At first I didn't totally trust myself with Greg. I knew his charm and smooth-talking ways could almost always get to me. But now, with things blossoming with Ben again, I knew Greg couldn't really turn my head no matter how suave he acted—and that was just it—it was all an act with him. Maybe I could actually go through with it. Maybe now was a good time to start. I tuned up the charm.

"Hey you, well right back atcha," I oozed. "Aren't you here all by your lonesome too?"

"No actually I was with Colleen and our new intern, Janie. They just left. I was paying the bill and about to head on back. But on second thought, you look like you could use some company."

Here we go.

"Maybe. I don't wanna hold you up, I mean if you need to get back to babysit." I just had to be a bitch. I needed to turn on the sweetness, not the witchy-poo.

"Very funny. Same old Abby. You seem irritated. I know just the thing for that," Greg said, pulling up a chair and sitting down across from me. His large frame and baby face just as adorable as ever. But I had a plan and I was sticking to it.

"You do? Well please, cast your spell and give me the tonic. I am having an agitating day. Nothing I can't handle of course."

"Of course," he raised his perfect eyebrow and grinned.

"So how are things with you," I pressed. "You said you have a new intern."

"Oh yeah, she's a grad student. Something Colleen set up. I thought we would take her out to lunch today to ease her in. She doesn't start officially until tomorrow."

"Oh well, you have enough work to have both an assistant and an intern. That's great." I bit my lip so I didn't say more. Like, *yeah all that work you're stealing from me.* I tried to be careful.

"Oh sure, you know, we've got stuff going on all the time," he bragged.

The waiter showed up, a long-haired boy with pimples on his forehead. Probably a freshman. I was a good girl and ordered sweet tea, no alcohol. Greg of course, ordered a cold Budweiser.

"Like what?" I chirped in a happy tone. "What's the next big thing you have going on over there?"

"Oh we're doing a little thing for Mother's Day. We've got a few things going on so I did actually need the help. Hey that Janie was sent through your old lovers department by the way." Greg smirked at me.

I played dumb. "Oh yeah, who do you mean? I had so many I can't even remember them all." I batted my eyes.

Greg giggled and nodded his head. "Touché." He toasted into the air then took a long swig of his just delivered Bud while staring a hole right through me. "Oh you'll have to get me up to speed sometime, but for now I'm referring to Mr. Ben Flannigan."

"Oh, Ben, that was so long ago. I barely remember." I shook my head and took a sip of my tea, looking directly into his dark brown eyes. I was ready to play and I was letting him know. "Tell me," I continued. "Are y'all doing that Mother's Day thing at a certain venue?"

"Well, I guess it's no big secret now. We're starting our campaign tomorrow and then everyone will know. It will be at the Jemison Mansion. Aren't y'all doing a Mother's Day thing too?"

"Oh uhm, yeah, well, it's not totally official yet." I suddenly became angered and was trying with all I had not to let it show. He knew damn good and well we had been planning something. He was so glib. Such a smart-ass. He was the one who grabbed my venue first, forcing me across the street to the smaller Friedman Home. Now I lost that today. I was so mad I felt like steam might seep out of my ears.

"Well you better get a move on it. It's just a few weeks

away."

I wanted in. I wanted to know everything. I felt like I would risk whatever I had to so Greg would fail. I was fuming but surely had to keep all that under wraps. He might see right through me.

"Well we do have a few little things we're working on but I have to keep things close to the chest if you know what I mean."

"I would love to know what that means," he grinned like the hungry fox about to eat Little Red Riding Hood. "How 'bout dinner tonight?"

"I have plans." I took another long sip of tea, teasing him while my blood boiled.

"Abby," he leaned in to get closer, "you look amazing. I've missed you. How 'bout we grab a bite to eat. Come on."

I leaned in to meet his gaze. We were inches apart. "I wish I could but tonight isn't good." I wanted to leave him hanging. Plus, I was so looking forward to seeing Ben.

And then the unimaginable happened! Oh no! Guess who walked in right behind Greg—Ben! At the very second Greg and I were only inches apart, it looked like we might kiss, I was sure. Ben glanced over and raised his dark eyebrows to me. I had just tuned down lunch with him, telling him I was busy, and now here I was with the arch nemesis! I was such a huge fool. And Ben had no idea that this was all part of the plan! I felt like I would throw up right in front of both of them.

I waved Ben over. He was with another man. Probably another one of his TAs. He smirked and shook his head. I waved harder. Greg noticed and turned around.

"Well, well, speak of the devil. There he is now. Hey Ben, get over here and join us," he bellowed.

My heart raced and I felt nauseated. I had no idea how to save myself. How to reassure Ben. What could I say without giving myself away? Ben let his companion know and the other man turned and trailed off to an open seat as Ben made his way around the chairs full of the lunch crowd and over to us. He looked confused, and I could see a little sadness in his eyes. I was sure he felt like I lied to him about my lunch plans.

"He there, Ben. Long time no see," Greg stood and stuck his hand out to Ben. They shook hands hard but Ben never looked at Greg. He stared straight into my eyes. I was sick inside. Mortified. Then I remembered. I had tried to call Ben to see if he could meet me. Surely he would have a missed call on his cell to back me up. That way he would at least know I wasn't lying to him when I told him I had too much to do and planned to not take lunch. But did I want Greg to know I had called Ben? He would surely get curious. I felt so trapped.

"I was just leaving," Greg offered unexpectedly. "Why don't y'all join in over here?" he suggested to Ben and his guest who had already taken a seat elsewhere. "Abby it was great seeing you," Greg continued. "Take care and uhm, good luck with that event. Oh and let me know if you're up for some dinner."

And there it was. Now Ben was sure to think I had been seeing Greg for a while—like we had dinner plans.

"Oh—well remember, I have plans for tonight, but maybe some other time," I smiled nervously.

"Here ya go, Ben." Greg stepped away from the table and pulled the chair out for Ben. "Y'all have a good lunch. Abby," Greg said as he turned to leave. "I'll be in touch." Greg winked and made his way back toward the front of the restaurant.

I leaned back in my chair and drew in a deep breath. Now—to clear things up with Ben. I just hoped he'd believe me. He knew my history with Greg so he would surely have reason not to.

CHAPTER FOURTEEN

Greg walked past Ben, patting him hard on the upper arm as he passed in front of him, heading toward the front of the little restaurant. "Good luck," I heard Greg say smirking and kinda under his breath. Ben grinned uncomfortably and then looked back at me. The confusion was clear in his perfect blue eyes. I could detect a tiny glint of sadness on his sweet face. I knew I had to talk to him.

"Come have a seat," I begged as I patted the table. I had already wiped up the condensation from Greg's glass and of course had put the dirty glass on the table behind me leaving a perfectly clean spot for Ben. OCD clean-freak always rears her head when I'm anxious. "Please," I pushed.

"I, uh, really need to get on back to my friend. I'll just call you later." Ben started to turn away.

"No, I need to say something. Sit down. Just for a minute," I insisted. I hit the table hard enough for the waiter to think I was demanding another drink. He headed over at a clip with his eyebrows arched.

"Okay," Ben agreed, "but just for a minute." He sat down and scooched in his chair just as the nervous waiter pulled out his order pad.

"More drinks I see, and you are new here," he motioned to

Ben. "What'll it be? Happy Hour all day on Tuesdays." He fidgeted and shifted his weight.

Ben was quiet.

I spoke up and ordered us both a sweet tea. The waiter nodded and left us alone. I reached across the table and laid my hand on Ben's forearm. "Ben, look at your phone," I insisted. "I tried to call when I suddenly decided to leave and grab lunch. I needed to get out of the station and get some air. I came here alone and Greg was already here. He was fixin' to leave when he saw me and came over to say hi. I promise. I didn't ditch your invitation so I could meet him."

"Uh huh, and what about your dinner plans? He seems to think you have some—at some point. Listen Abby, a lot of years have passed and really if you still need Greg in your life you gotta just be honest. It's been like this forever and I just don't play second place too well anymore."

"No, I swear. I have nothing for him. He may want to see me but I told him I had plans for tonight—cause I thought I did—with you." My heart was racing and my eyes began to sting with the first drops of tears. I was just exhausted.

"Abby, you were leaning into him. Your faces were inches apart."

"It's an act. It's all part of my plan. The entire scheme to undo Greg Galloway once and for all. I didn't tell you about it yet but it goes along with the intern you sent and my working with Cate. Please. I swear. It was just part of my plan." I drew in a deep breath and leaned back as the sweet tea arrived.

"Alrighty, y'all, here we go. Don't get too crazy with all that sugar," he giggled as het set the teas down in front of us.

I gave him the stink-eye. I had no tolerance for happy talk at that moment—on that *day* actually. Starting off with my deranged neighbor, then my assistant idiot Cate and now this. I was frazzled. I knew Ben could tell. He saw me give the waiter the evil eye and grinned, taking his phone from his pocket to look for my missed call. He looked up at me.

"Abby, I see you tried to call. Just calm down. I can't even imagine what all has been going on today. I'm sorry I doubted you. Are you okay?"

Ben leaned in and placed his hand over mine. I took in a breath and let it out nodding my head. "Come on over to my table and join us. You clearly haven't eaten. I'd love for you to meet Dillon. He's a first year TA—really cool. We can chitchat and not get into anything—you know, just keep it light. You need to eat. Come on."

Ben didn't give me a chance to answer. He gripped my hand and got up, still holding onto me and pulled me across the restaurant to his table with Dillon. I felt relieved. I just needed to let down. Keep it light I repeated to myself. Just as I took my seat and the introductions were made between Dillon and me, I glanced back at our table where the waiter was now giving me the stink-eye. He shrugged his shoulders and shook his head as he took the teas and pranced over to us.

"I can wait this table too, Miss. Let me know when you're ready." He turned to leave as Dillon spoke up.

"Uhm, I'll just have water with lemon," he smiled.

"Well, my heavens aren't you the life of the party?" The waiter smirked and headed off toward the kitchen.

Lunch was easy, as most things were with Ben. He paid for me and Dillon and we stood outside on the sidewalk just as Dillon shook his hand and said goodbye, leaving Ben and me alone in the early afternoon sunshine in the middle of the downtown sidewalk. Ben looked down and shoved his hands into his front pockets. He was adorable. He looked up at me and smiled a small grin. I smiled back at him.

"Feel better? He asked.

"I do, thank you. And thank you for being so understanding. I feel like I need a lot of that these days."

"It's okay. I know this isn't college anymore, and I also know your history with Greg. Abby, seriously, just be careful."

"Of what?"

Ben suddenly stepped closer to me and placed his hands on my shoulders. He looked so serious, almost worried. "Of the whole situation. I'm not stupid. Greg is still Greg. Just be careful, that's all I'm saying."

"Be careful of what?"

"Greg—Greg himself. I know you know what I mean. Right?"

I looked at Ben. What was he trying to say to me? Maybe he didn't trust Greg, but I had a feeling he didn't trust me either.

"Do you think he's dangerous for me? Are you not sure of my feelings for you? C'mon Ben. Seriously. We've been down this road before," I pleaded.

"Exactly my point. I know he has some sort of hold over you. I've seen him with you and watched you with him and you can say it all day long that you can't stand him but in the end he can have you if he wants you. This is a dangerous game you're playing, Abby. Just watch yourself. I don't want you hurt."

Ben was sincere, but it really upset me. I knew now he didn't fully trust me and this was the worst possible way to start a new relationship.

"I don't even know what to say to that, Ben. Greg and I were over way back in college." Of course, no one knew about two years ago at the broadcasters convention, but that was my secret. "You have to trust me for this to be real for us. I know what I'm doing," I promised.

But did I? I thought so but maybe I was wrong. I hugged Ben goodbye and gave him a reassuring smile.

"Still on for dinner?" He asked innocently.

"Of course. Why don't you pick up something and come to my house? I'll be home around six."

"What would you like?"

"Surprise me." I blew him a kiss and turned to make my way down the sidewalk to my car. I felt a little sadness stirring in the pit of my stomach. I knew if I stopped long enough to make one of my lists about the perfect man to spend the rest of my life with it would be all Ben. He was the perfect man. He always had been. I was just too wrapped up in my career to see it. Maybe I did see it and it scared me. He was so settled and secure in himself. But the thing was, over the years I had grown up and I could see a rare second chance with the one that got away and I knew it was what I wanted. But clearly Ben had trust issues with me. Oh, I didn't blame him at all. I knew I would have to take it slow so his trust in me could grow and I had to earn every single ounce of it. But I was willing to work for what I knew could be something really special. If only I didn't screw it all up before it ever got off the ground.

CHAPTER FIFTEEN

I pulled into my driveway at exactly five minutes before six. Ben had called and said he would meet me here with our dinner. Al Roker was pacing around my porch and sniffing the azaleas still scattered all around. Al Roker was Mitzy's yellow Persian cat. He was always after Gertrude. I turned off my car and made my way up the steps. Al Roker wasn't a nice kitty. He was usually angry, pushy and demanding, just like his narcissistic owner. Gertie was sprawled out in the window just teasing Al. She knew exactly what she was doing and who had all the power to drive that man kitty crazy. A cat after my own heart. As I carefully placed my feet so as not to step on the plants, dirt or Mr. Roker, a note fell from my screen door. I knew it was a threat for my deranged neighbor. I pushed my way inside, and promptly tripped over Mitzy's mailbox. I had forgotten I had yanked it from the red dirt and dropped it in my living room. "Ow, ow ow," I yelped as I hopped on my one good foot. I knew that would leave a mark not to mention what a mess it had made of my perfect red pedicure.

Damn Mitzy! She *made* me take that hideous mailbox!

I squatted over it and heaved it up from the floor, dragging it to my hall closet as I limped across the dining room. Ben would be coming soon and I had no way to explain the mailbox laying like a dead dog inside my front door still covered in red dirt. Ben thought he couldn't trust me with Greg—I hated to know what he'd think of me stealing my neighbor's mailbox. He might have me committed. I pushed the closet door closed but it wouldn't latch. The mailbox was too big. I closed it and stuck a chair in front of the door to keep it from creeping open.

I limped back to the front room and looked at my fat grey kitty on the back of the couch. She was still meowing at Al Roker.

"Hi Miss Gertrude," I said sweetly. "It's not nice to tease the men you know?" I shook my head at the irony of my scheme with Greg. I took my car keys from my pocket threw them on the antique credenza just inside the door and flicked on the lamp. Kicking off my pumps I dropped my purse down on the over-stuffed floral sofa and plopped down with Gertrude just above my head. It was always her favorite place to sit, just above my head. Every so often she would butt her head against mine to let me know she loved me. Or wanted me to rub her. I could hear her purring as I opened that letter that had been in my screened door.

Dear Ms. Harper,

It has come to my attention that you may need my help. Though you don't know whom this letter is from at the moment, I assure you that one day you will. We have a lot in common, you and I. In the coming days I will be sending you notes so that you will know you are not alone in your battles. I will be fighting in secret right along side you. One day you will know the truth and know why I have done all the things I plan to do in the next few weeks. Just know you have a silent sister out here and I am on your side.

Sincerely,

Secret Sister.

What. The. Hell? I sat up straight up on the couch as Gertie butted my head. Al Roker was still screeching just outside the window wanting to pounce on my Gertrude. *Secret Sister? Help me?* This actually scared me. My heart quickened.

I suddenly was worried someone besides Al was on my porch watching me. A secret sister? My mouth went dry as I swallowed hard. Ben was on his way and I was still in my suit, my toenail chipped, red dirt all over my foyer, and just as I was obsessing, the phone rang.

"Hello?"

"Well, hey Zelda, it's Flannery O'Conner! You know," she whispered. "Dixie Darlene. I'm using my book club name."

"Oh yes, Flannery, how are things?" I asked trying to sound perky. Like my foot wasn't swelling and there wasn't a crazed cat with the name of a famous weatherman yelling his head off on my porch wanting to screw the bejeezus out of my cat, like there wasn't a bunch of pink azaleas with their root balls still attached strewn all over my front porch, oh and like there wasn't a stolen full sized US mailbox propped in my coat closet. And now I have a stalker who likes to call herself, Secret Sister! Yes, hello Flannery you idiot, you know your name is Dixie and you will never ever be Flannery but go right ahead and live in your strange little fantasy world. I will join you only if you promise to hang up in thirty seconds flat.

"I'm so glad I caught you," she chattered. "I just wanted to make sure you got my message from earlier. I left it on your voicemail."

No, Flannery. I have not listened to my messages yet, I've been saving my cat from a rape and hiding stolen federal property. You know—just a boring little evening here doing the same old same old, I thought to myself.

"No, not yet," I stammered. "Just walking in."

"Okey Dokey girl, no problem. I just wanted you to know Book Club has been permanently moved to Thursdays. Seems like we may get a better turn-out. Friday's just no good for everyone. Who knew?"

See? You'll never be Flannery! You are too stupid!

"Yeah sounds good –I'll be there." Her thirty seconds had quickly swished by and she only had ten seconds left. I held my wrist so I could see the second hand on my antique Cartier watch. 8, 7, 6...

"Oh, and honey, don't forget you have doughnut duty..."

3, 2,...

"Oh dear someone's at my door. Bye Flannery!" I clicked the kitchen phone down and limped to the fridge, flung open the door and swigged down my bottle of mimosa. God help me, I am in the middle of a circus.

Just then the doorbell rang. I quickly glanced at the front hall closet door to make sure the mailbox was outta site. I wiped my mouth with my sleeve, then took off my suit jacket and threw it over the back of a kitchen chair. I poofed my hair and checked myself in the side of the toaster like a mirror. I then wiped my teeth with my index finger and limped to the door feeling like I was totally pathetic. I flung open the door to see Ben standing there with my old college favorite—Taco Casa. I smiled and he grinned back at me.

"You said to surprise you and I know we survived on this in college. I hoped it might hit the spot after the way things had been going today. Whadya think?"

I seriously wanted to jump into his arms.

"It's so perfect! Get in here and lets eat. You had to be reading my mind. This is just what I needed," I gushed as I closed the door behind him. I led the way to the kitchen, still limping.

"Dare I ask why you are limping?" Ben asked as we made our way to the kitchen table.

"Oh, uhm, I tripped over Gertrude when I walked in. Just tired I'm sure." I tried to brush it off.

"Oh, I thought you might have stumbled over all those plants. It looks like you had a war with some azaleas, and the shrubs won big time," he laughed. "The porch is so covered in dirt. I'll clean it up after dinner but I'm here if you need to talk about why you got so mad at those pink bushes."

We both sat down at the round wooden table in my cozy kitchen. We opened the sacks of perfect burritos, mild for me and extra hot for Ben, frijoles and sanchos followed by the perfectly crispy sopapillas. I was full and satisfied. I had totally embarrassed myself eating like a teenaged boy and shoveling chips and salsa into my face at lightening speed. My perfectly controlled uber clean life was falling apart right before my eyes. Suddenly things became overwhelming. I looked down and I had dripped sauce down my perfectly pressed white Ann Taylor blouse. My hair was hanging in my face. I was one hot mess.

"Abby, I know you have so much going on and with the look of your war-torn porch there has to be even more than I know. I need to tell you now, you don't have to always be so perfect, so controlled with me. It's a little annoying. The only real fault I can find," he smiled. "It's okay to let yourself lean on someone every once in a while. You can always lean on me, you know that. Tell me what is swirling around in the pretty head tonight. I can see the frustration and I'm here for you."

Ben was so cute and genuine. And yes, I was very certain about how annoying I was—much of the time. I wanted to tell him everything, even about that note that was freaking me out from a supposed secret sister. But I felt like I would just be a huge wimpy whiner. That wasn't me. People always thought of me as strong, the one in control, the organizer. But now look at me. I had hit the proverbial wall. I glanced up at Ben and felt tears sting my eyes. I wanted to talk, but mostly I *needed* to talk. Men don't like drama queens. My mother, Toots, was the biggest drama queen in the family and maybe I was subconsciously trying like hell not to be like her. I knew men wouldn't like all that out of control behavior of a drama queen so I never became one. I left that title to my sisters and to my insane mother, Toots. Lord at the drama they created. I was always the one who put the fire out. I was going to be my usual self and hold it all in but the tears fell and before I knew it I was talking.

"Ben I'm so sorry. I don't want to burden you. I'm sure you have enough on your plate these days without all my stuff." I sniffed and wiped the runaway tear.

"Abby, we're friends, more than friends. I'm here for you. C'mon, lemme help if I can. Why don't we just leave all this and go into the living room. It looks like you need some comfort, and you can put that hurt ankle up for while. C'mon, I'll help you." It was seriously bothering me to leave all that fast food paper and dirty napkins all over the table. This went completely against my OCD tidy nature. But I went along looking at the big mess of paper on my table. I grabbed a few pieces and shoved them in the trashcan by the sink. I just couldn't leave a mess. Even if I wanted to.

Ben shook his head and grinned. "Still a clean-freak, annoying, again, but cute."

Ben slid his chair back and stood over me and slipped his forearm under my arm, and held my waste with his other hand around my back. I hobbled back, then limped a few steps over near that front hall closet and tried to put some weight on my right ankle. "Ouch! I think I may need some ice for it."

"Okay let me get it," Ben said and left me standing on my bad ankle for one too many seconds. I began to hobble to the chair that was blocking the closet door so the mailbox wouldn't fall out. I limped one step and reached for the chair—and missed it. I grabbed the seat as I fell forward. I hit the floor, pulling the chair as I went. As the chair dragged forward the closet door crept open and in slow motion the mailbox fell out right on top of me. So here I was, lying on my wooden hall floor with a chair and a full-sized US mailbox on top of me.

"Oh my God! What the hell? Abby! Are you okay?" Ben screeched as he dropped the ice pack he was making and leapt over to me, throwing the mailbox then the chair to the side and helping me sit up.

"Oh Ben, see? I told you I had too much on my plate right now."

"Please tell me the *too much* thing has something to do with this mailbox."

"I was going to tell you. I was. Just get me to the couch. Get me that ice and I promise you'll know everything. Whether you'll want to stay here after I tell you all this crap is totally another thing."

Hmm, that sounded a little bossy. Maybe I'm still in here somewhere.

"Hang on to me, I gotcha," Ben ordered.

Ben scooped me up in his arms and carried me Officer And A Gentleman style to the couch and laid me down. "Stay here," he commanded.

Ben left and returned with the ice pack and laid it gently across my swollen ankle. He slowly lifted my legs and sat down under them, letting my legs fall across his lap. It was heavenly. "Okay," he began, "Now tell Dr. Flannigan everything."

"Dr. Flannigan," I smiled. "You *are* Dr. Flannigan! PhD! I've been wanting to say it since we bumped into each other last week. I love it. Okay let me see…where do I start?" Ben did have his communication doctorate so it was in fact true. My feet were being cared for by a Doctor. I told Ben how sorry I was for not telling him about my plans with Greg, and then all about Cate the idiot. I finally worked my way to Mitzy. And her mailbox.

"You cannot be serious," Ben popped. "You know that is federal property."

"I know. I have no idea what has gotten into me. I am suddenly a crazed lunatic. None of this is like me but that Mitzy tells me she is a life coach and I dress like Hilary Clinton, who actually dresses like Kim Jong-un of North Korea. So I dress like a stocky dictator. I'm losing it, Ben."

"No, you're just going through too much at one time. Stuff like this makes us do crazy things."

Ben was softly caressing my legs, slipping his hands under my pant-legs and kneading my skin in his warm hands. It felt delicious and made me relax.

"We can handle all of this. I will get someone to replant all those azaleas if you want me to. We can move them all to the front along the sidewalk. I think that would work. You have to return the mailbox. I will re-plant that too. There's nothing here that's life or death or that we can't handle. Okay?" Ben was reassuring and soothing. I drew in a deep breath and nodded as he massaged my feet. Ben was good. Just good to his soul. He was hard to take because he never had any ulterior motives. He just simply wanted to love and be loved. Some women considered that boring. He was fun and funny too but mostly he just loved to love. He wasn't that bad boy on a big ass motorcycle revving his engines. He was that guy in his vintage little red Triumph. He was that guy who collected vintage cars and racehorses. It was a total turn-on.

I stared at him as he comforted me in the dimly lit room, my floral printed sofa awash in the amber glow of the evening. Ben had opened the front windows and the music of the late spring symphony floated around outside. Crickets hummed and birds cooed. The bush frogs added the rhythm. A cool evening breeze caught the current and drifted inside bringing with it the fragrance of the ten azalea bushes still lying on the craftsman style oversized porch. It was a magical moment. But would it last? Ben was sincere but I wasn't so sure I would ever allow myself to be vulnerable enough to really let anyone inside. I knew if I was really going to have this second chance with Ben I had to. I just wasn't so sure I could.

CHAPTER SIXTEEN

The evening passed and the talking became easier and more satisfying. I felt safe with Ben. The problem was me. I was afraid to let anyone see me at my worst. I was always so careful to be professional and classy and I watched myself, kept myself in check at all times. But in the last week or two I had felt myself coming undone. I think I had held myself too tightly for so long that I was bursting inside. I longed to feel secure enough to be okay with spilled sauce on my blouse, or dirt on my floors and a fancy flouncy dress once in a while. I was so tightly wound I felt like I was choking myself. I needed to feel Ben next to me. I longed for him but it was so strange. Two years ago when I was with Greg I was totally in control. It was just pleasures of the flesh and nothing more. I decided to have sex with him. I remember making that decision. Greg didn't coax me.

With Ben it was so much more complicated. It was emotional. It made me vulnerable and needy and I wasn't comfortable with that. But I so wanted it. Wanted him, just all of him right that second.

I reached out my arms to Ben and he leaned sideways next to me. He scooched up the back of the couch until he was face to face with me, his head lying on my breast. I ran my hands through his thick dark hair as he began to nuzzle my neck. I felt his lips on the skin beneath my jaw, nibbling and tasting me. He pulled up and looked at me softly, his blue eyes catching the glow of the porch light, he closed them as he pressed his perfect mouth on mine. Here I was with an ice pack on my ankle and burrito sauce on my shirt and Ben was kissing me like I was the only woman in the world. His weight partially on top of me felt so wonderful. He was long and lean and broad shouldered and so manly. And he smelled wonderful. I kissed him back passionately, under his neck, on his cheeks, devouring him in my arms. This felt different than college. There was something about him, something so confident.

I had never allowed myself to lean on anyone. Especially not a man and never fully. I didn't want to be one of those girls that needed her man to function. Like a child needing permission and being dependent was most certainly not in my description of the woman I knew I was. I guess I never allowed myself to feel vulnerable. It made me feel weak and when I felt even a tinge of that I cringed in disgust. It made me think of my mother. Toots was the definition of weak. She had an affair with my dad's brother before I was born and my oldest sister Rhonda was the result. I never wanted to be anything but exactly who I became, smart and strong and independent.

But I felt my walls coming down that night with Ben lying next to me on my couch, his long slender fingers wandering the contours of my body. I allowed him to break through and love me. And it felt so scrumptious. He continued to kiss and caress me, his hands unbuttoning my blouse, slowly, deliberately. My hands reaching into his tan corduroys and freeing his shirttail, allowing me access underneath it to his tan warm flesh. My fingers mapped his muscular back and perfect frame as he kissed the tops of my breasts that spilled from my lacey pale pink bra.

Ben stopped to gaze into my eyes as if asking permission. I closed my eyes and arched my head back giving him the approval he needed. Ben adjusted himself a little lower kissing my abdomen as I pulled gently at his hair. I could feel his wavy dark mane dragging along my ribs as he worked his way to my pants, unbuttoning them as he kissed my skin on his way down.

I pulled at his shirt until it was over his head, taking it completely off and dropping it to the floor. Ben tugged at my pants and I helped him wriggling so he could pull them down exposing my perfect matching lace panties. He glanced up and smiled at me. My heart was racing with the thrill of him, his warm lips, his perfect body, and the simple fact that it was me he wanted. It was so easy to be back in this place—the place we had known so well together once upon a time. I felt my pants slide down and drop to the floor as Ben repositioned himself on top of me. He was on his knees straddling me as I unbuttoned his pants and he helped me pull them down around his fabulous hot thighs. I slipped my hands into his dark boxer briefs and held his manhood in my hands—just as we heard a siren outside.

A flash of light hit the front windows and Ben dropped down on top of me.

He laughed for a split second before he spoke. "Uhm I think someone wants their mailbox back."

CHAPTER SEVENTEEN

Ben rolled off of me and grabbed his pants, slipping them over his butt while he lay on the bare floor. He reached over and grabbed his T-shirt that had come off inside his button-down when I pulled it over his head and put it back on. I was completely indisposed with my stained blouse open and nothing but my lacey pink panties on for pants.

Ben looked at me and shook his head, code to be quiet. He would answer the cops at the door. I lay as still as possible. Soon, the doorbell chimed.

Ben opened the door.

"Evening officers what can I do for you?" He was calm.

"Evening sir. We got a call 'bout a stolen mailbox. The lady seems to think it might be over here."

"Oh really? She never said a thing to us about it." Ben continued the act.

"Welp, she's pretty sure. Says she got this letter this morning on her porch and says it's from the lady who owns this house."

Oh God. I knew I had to do something. But what? I would incriminate myself. I could lie. I had gotten good at that when I used to have to lie for my mother. But just as I was trying to move to get my pants, Ben spoke up.

"Let me see that," he ordered reaching his hand out to hold the letter.

"No, I don't recognize that hand writing at all. Hmm, that letter says that the person has the mailbox, but it doesn't say where that person lives. I believe it to be a prank and that signature doesn't belong to anyone I know. But, hey, we'll keep an eye out. Our mailbox may be next who knows?"

"Looks like all these flowers here may be what she was talking about having replaced in that little note," I heard the other officer point out.

Someone in the HOA left those for us to plant along the sidewalk. I had accidentally planted them along the property line. I'll have that taken care of first thing. Hey it could be a disgruntled member of the HOA for that matter."

"Is the owner here?"

"No, I'm house-sitting for her. She has a cat and I'm taking care of things. She's out of town."

"Okay well y'all be careful. If somebody's out there taking mailboxes you could be next. Have a good night."

I heard the officers' shoes walk away as Ben shut the door. Ben pulled the blinds as I rolled off the couch and crawled toward the kitchen. Ben followed me. I stopped right in front of the mailbox in the front hallway.

"God, Ben you lied for me. Did you take an improv class that I never knew about?"

"Abby this is serious. I'm gonna get that mailbox back where it goes tonight."

"Ben, again, do you realize you lied to the police? You could be in big trouble if they catch you."

"I knew what I was doing. I was protecting you and I did what I had to do to make sure you were safe. I know you had to have not been in your right mind when you ripped the mailbox from the ground. How you even did that is beyond me. I didn't really lie. I could be housesitting. I don't have to admit I know your handwriting. Maybe it was too dark to see it. No matter what, I am getting this back tonight and we're getting those plants re-planted. It will be okay."

"Sorry about tonight," I muttered. "I surely had better plans than crawling to the kitchen on my hands and knees in my undies."

Ben smiled and scooted over to me. He leaned over. "You were sexy as hell. I enjoyed watching it."

I laughed. "Well right back atcha. Let me button this shirt and get the kitchen cleaned up," I said changing the subject.

The kitchen was clean and the full moon shone through the windows over the sink. I gazed out and looked up to the left searching the skies for Orion. I felt Ben slip his hands around my waist and pull me backwards into him. He put his lips near my ear and whispered, "Lets go outside and make a wish."

"My thoughts exactly," I agreed.

Ben laced his fingers through mine and led the way outside through the back screened porch and into my lush back yard. There was a clearing in the back right corner and I had put Adirondack chairs just for stargazing. I led the way to the chairs and we both took a seat. The warm air was relaxing and not too humid. A rare time in the Deep South. Fragrant evening air filled us with the intoxicating perfume of magnolia coming from the large silky blossoms that hung overhead. I leaned back and searched the night sky for my little cluster of stars, Pleiades. So faint, barely visible, it was mysterious.

I remember lying for hours on summer nights on the grass at my Granny Cartwright's with my sisters. They would get bored and go in long before me. When I would feel lonely or insecure I would look for Pleiades and know all was right in the world. Nothing bad had happened and I was safe right where I was. I know it was this anxiety that made me a neat freak and wound me up tighter than turkey twine. Pleiades was always right there watching over me and providing a guiding light into the sometimes-scary night. I felt the weight of the world on me at times. Annie was more emotional, always wearing her feelings on the outside. Getting those feelings out whenever she needed to, never worrying what anyone thought.

Rhonda was always cooking with Granny and my mom was almost always gone. She would say it was for long weekends at the Gulf with her friends but we found out a couple of years ago, she had been with my uncle Ron, my Daddy's brother. I always suspected she was not with her girlfriends. I think we all did. And I tried to carry the heavy weight of the unspoken glances I'd catch between the two of them and the whispers that drifted up the hall in the middle of the night. I knew Rhonda was strong and she was the oldest, but I was always the most serious.

We were all believers in magic though, the magic of secret wishes. Rhonda always wished on dandelions. She and Granny would sit on the porch of the old stately plantation home that had been in the family for centuries and make wishes on the dandelions growing on the side yard. Annie loved to lay in her little bed of clover and say she was looking for her future husband. Her little dream was that if she found a four-leafed one, that on that day, twenty years from then, she would marry her prince.

I was the astronomer, always searching the heavens for a falling star to make my wish. Always wishing for the exact same thing—safety, security, and love.

It was sad in a way, hopeful in another.

I sat there that night gazing upwards with Ben right next to me and wondered if maybe he might be made of stardust, like a comet returning back to me after so many years. I watched him as he sat still, the blue moon-shadows dancing across his perfectly chiseled symmetrical face and thought of my self as a young teenager looking for my constellation and squinting my eyes shut wishing the nights away. Looking at Ben made me think for the first time that maybe it was all really possible, to have security and love and safety all in one person—and that maybe I could actually share myself with someone.

"Hey! Look! A shooting star," Ben called out in the silence. "Hurry, make a wish!"

I closed my eyes tight and made my wish. When I opened

them Ben was standing right in front of me, a smile on his face. The question was, had I always been in the way of my own wishes coming true? It was looking more like it every single day. I knew I needed to get out of my own way. But how? That was the question of a lifetime.

CHAPTER EIGHTEEN

Midnight came and Ben took the mailbox back to Mitzy's yard and re-planted it. The hole was still there and he took a bucket of water to make it muddy so it would hold and buried it back into the red dirt. He wore an old black hoodie I had that once belonged to Daddy so he wouldn't be seen. He ran to my backyard and entered in through the back door to stay hidden. He kissed me goodnight and I let him out through the front door in his own clothes.

It was late and we both had to work the next day and it had certainly been a long night. I was still silently fuming that Mitzy had the nerve to send the freaking police to my house. I wasn't through with her and though everything in me told me to just let it all go now I couldn't help myself. I had to write her another note so I could get it all off my chest before I went to bed.

Dear Mitzy,

Sending the cops here was quite ballsy of you. Did your life coach handbook instruct you to do that? I bet so. Seriously Mitz who do you think you are? I am no more criminal than you—as you'll recall, you have committed vandalism and the cops were asking me about why all those footballed azaleas were all over my porch. I was within a gnat's eyelash of *turning you in for vandalism. But I decided not to stoop to your low level. But now, I will give you a deadline. I am quite certain that as a life coach, you work well under deadline pressure. You have until TODAY by six o'clock to turn that shared alleyway into a garden as it once was or tomorrow night Mitz, you better have some doughnuts because the Tuscaloosa PD will be investigating you for a vandalism charge. I also have it in your handwriting that you removed the azaleas and left them on my porch. You admit it Mitzy in **your own hand**. I am very delighted at your honesty.*

By the way, that oversized cat of yours tried all night to rape my Gertrude so I would appreciate it if you could keep him on your side of the shared alley. If not you may need to check with the local shelter for Al Roker.

Remember Mitz, six o'clock tomorrow night. Oh and just in case, Krispy Kreme has the dozen size boxes two for one right now.

Sincerely,
The Azalea Queen

I threw on the black hoodie and ran across the alley to Mitzy's porch and dropped the note at her front door. Al Roker was in the window and meowed from inside the house at me. I high-tailed it back to my house and snuck inside, all the lights already off. There. It was done. Hopefully Al Roker didn't give me away.

I smiled to myself as I crawled into bed and turned off the light. Ben's after shave was still on my skin and I felt his weight on me all night long. I knew I had to trust myself and let him in. but when push came to shove, would I?

* * *

I arrived at work and went straight to my office from the back parking lot. Cate wasn't there yet and I actually felt relieved. I closed my door for a few minutes of peace before the charade of spying on Greg would take up most of this day.

Annie, Cate and I were going out to the Battle- Friedman Home to check the venue for the Mother's Day event. It would be here before I knew it and somehow I wanted to go out on top. I knew I needed a change and the truth was I had a good savings. Enough for me to take some time off and see if I wanted to do something else with my miserable life. That was my plan anyway until I ran into Ben. Still, I wanted to out-do Greg and we needed a plan. Annie had called her friend at the Battle- Friedman Home and made us an appointment. Cate had insisted she wanted to go and that over made-up station manager Toni Lyn butted in with *"hey that's a great idea, she can take some pictures."* So yep—Cate was coming too. Toni Lyn Tingle herself even wanted to come but I told her too many people at one time might make things more awkward. We were going to ask for a favor and I didn't want Annie's friend to feel like she was under too much pressure.

I plopped down on the loveseat under the oversized window in my office. This station was housed in a historic home from the early 1800s. It had been saved a few years back by Lewis and turned into the Crimson Tide Sports Network. He was so careful to restore it and not renovate it. The dark walnut floors were original and the whole place appealed to my intense love of history. I heard my cell phone buzz me with a text message. I rummaged through my bag with my hand and felt the hard side of my phone. When I pulled it out though, my hand also held the note from Secret Sister I got last night. With all the intimacy developing between Ben and me, I had totally forgotten it. My stomach dropped as I realized what I held in my hand.

I read my text. It was Ben. *Last night was unforgettable.*

I wrote him back, *Which part? The mailbox or the cops?* I put a smiley face and a heart.

Neither, what comes to mind is you crawling to the kitchen in your undies and sitting in the back yard with you wishing on a falling star. See you tonight?

You really want more of that? I teased.

Much more! He put a smiley face.

See you at six? I asked.

Let's go get some dinner and then we can come over to my house tonight? He asked.

Perfect. I'll meet you at your office.

He sent back another smiley. I relaxed back into the couch still clutching that mysterious letter from someone who called herself Secret Sister. I had gotten it last night just as I got home. But then all the fun began. Well, fun with Ben anyway.

Who could it be sending me this note? I wondered. My nature was to decipher the possibilities. Ben had calmed me so much last night that I felt a little more in control for the first time in a week. I knew that old me, the list-maker would be needed today so I tried not to think of Greg, or Mitzy. I started thinking. It was from someone who would know what was going on in my personal life. I wasn't sure if the note was referring to helping with Greg or with my deranged neighbor. But it was someone who knew. The fact was no one knew about Mitzy except Ben now. So it had to be from someone who knew about the situation with Greg. Annie knew. But I was sure it wasn't from her and I was also sure no one else knew.

Just then Cate pushed open my door.

"Oh my word, you scared the livin' daylights outta me. I had no idea you were here already," Cate said in a startled voice.

"Honey, let me clue you in—knocking is a good thing and proper etiquette."

"Oh, I'm sorry. I just wanted to give you this note. It was a message that came in on voicemail last night right after you left. I thought I would write it down on this sticky note thing and attach it to your computer."

"What—what is it? Just hand it to me. You don't have to stick it to the computer now, I'm right here." Was it really possible to be such a dumbass?

Cate handed me the sticky note. *"Hey Abs, let me take you*

to dinner tonight. I have the perfect new place. Lemme know."
I quickly read the senders name.
Greg Galloway.
He was his usual pushy self. The problem was this was my scheme to rope him in and get his secrets. But it looked like he was back on top, scheming to rope me first. Could it be? Surely not. His depth of scheming was not that sophisticated. If I accept then I have to break with Ben for tonight, I thought. But, if I give an alternative date to Greg, then I'm back in the lead position. I went to my desk and sent Mr. Galloway an email.
Hey Greg,
Plans for tonight but I'm free tomorrow. Name the time and place and I'll be there.
Abby

Just as I hit send, Annie popped into my office. "Morning honey, how goes it? We still on for lunch and the Battle-Friedman Home? I can't wait! I talked to Jeanette when I went by yesterday. She said she never spoke to you and we are still booked for Mother's Day."
"What? Why didn't you call me?"
"Well, I told you Matt was coming home and we had, uhm, a little home-coming. It lasted into the wee hours so I just thought I'd tell you now."
I had to stop and think for a minute to put all this together.
"Annie, I called the venue myself and they told me they were booked."
"Well, Jeanette is the only one who books the place and I swear she said she never spoke to you. But look, the good news is that we still have the place for the event. No worries and no need to panic. Are we still going there today to look over the place?"
Annie stood before me in her hot pink sling backs and white vintage dress. It was covered in pink peonies and pale green hydrangea blossoms. She had done a billboard in this ensemble for her friend CarolAnn's vintage dress shop. She

looked like the star she was. She had an innocence and zest for life. Not much ever got her down. I was the polar opposite—on every level. Annie trusted everyone, I trusted no one. And right that second, I smelled a big rat. I knew I returned the call and I knew I had spoken to someone who told me not to get snarky with her. That same person had told me the Battle- Friedman Home was booked on Mother's Day. I knew someone was up to no good and I was suddenly determined to find out who was behind that fake phone call.

CHAPTER NINETEEN

Annie got up to leave my office and head downstairs to prep for her show. She had some promos to do and a commercial to voice before she hit the air.

"Okay I'll meet you in the lobby after I get off the air," she said as she headed to the door then turned dramatically. "Open, closed? You never know," she smirked.

"Open." I popped.

She shrugged and turned, her dress flouncing as she made her way past Cate and down the back staircase.

I leaned back in my chair after she left and tried to piece together the new mystery surrounding my event. Someone called and spoke to Cate. Cate took the message and handed me the note with a number. I called the number and the lady on the other end told me I could not have the venue. Okay—so either Cate was lying but she had to be in cahoots with the person who answered the phone or Cate could be in the clear, and the phone call itself was a fake. But why? And Who? So many questions, my head was spinning.

I went through my garbage can under my desk. The cleaning crew comes in once a week so that post-it note should still be in there. I got down on my hands and knees and went under my desk to retrieve the note. Sifting through the can I came across the hot pink sticky note and just as I was pulling it out of the can,

"Oh my word, what are you doing under there?" Toni Lyn Tingle's voice echoed overhead as I came face to face with her hot pink toes.

I popped up so quickly I banged my head. "Ow!" I screeched as I tried to stand up. Toni Lyn didn't need to know a thing about all this. She was just a busy body and I wanted to handle this on my own.

"Lord girl that's gonna leave a mark. What in hell are you doing?"

"Oh nothing, it's part of my morning exercises to crawl around under my desk. Good for the heart rate."

"Oh honey, you're a hoot. What'd you lose, an earring?

"Yep that's it. I got it." I slipped my hand under my hair and pulled my pearl clip earring off and held it out for Toni Lyn to see.

"Good. Glad you found it, honey. But even if you hadn't those are so common they'd be easy to replace."

I pursed my lips together so I wouldn't say something that could get me fired. Instead I changed the subject. "Can I help you? Did you need to see me?" I asked clipping my earring back on while I was standing up.

"I just wanted to make sure you were still going out to the Battle- Friedman Home this afternoon. I had so wanted to go but I have a meeting out of the office I can't get out of."

"Yep we're all set to go. I'll let you know the details tomorrow. We are hoping to take pictures so you can see what we're planning." I was trying so hard to be nice but all I wanted was for her to leave so I could look at the phone number on the sticky-note.

"Great. Okay well have a blast and I'll see you tomorrow for the full report," Toni Lyn clapped her hands together, putting an exclamation point on her remark and turned to walk out. She was trying to do her job as station manager but really did we even need her? I walked over and pushed my door closed. I saw Cate's purse on her desk so I knew she was finally at work. I also knew I didn't want her to hear me in case she was involved. I went back to my desk and looked at the number on the sticky-note. Then I immediately looked up the number to the Battle- Friedman Home. Not the same number. I looked at all the contact numbers for the venue—nothing resembling the number on the sticky-note. I wondered if the number belonged to a cell phone. I took a deep breath and decided to call the number on the note. I knew if I called from the station it would give me away. So I decided to call from my own cell phone. My heart raced as I pushed in the number on my cell.

Two rings, nothing. Then finally, "Hey this is Serena, leave me a message." I hung up. I had to think. This was certainly not the voice of the woman I called the day before. I wanted to ask Cate a few questions but surely didn't want her to catch on just in case. I'd rather catch her in the act if she happened to be involved.

I had so much to tell Annie about all my plans with Ben but since Cate was going with us to the Battle- Friedman Home, I knew it wouldn't happen. I looked at the note again. There was no name, just the phone number. That was odd and it was something I could ask Cate about to see if she squirms.

"Cate, could you come in here for a minute?" I threw my voice out to the upstairs landing where she was at her desk.

"Sure," she yelped.

Cate stepped in front of my desk. I played it sweet and innocent.

"I was just looking at this number you gave me and I wanted to call this lady back but I didn't see a name. Did you get her name by any chance?"

Cate took the note and stared at it. She shook her head. "Oh no, I'm so sorry. I'm sure she must've said her name but I guess I didn't write it down. Oh Miss Harper I really want this job but so far I'm crashing and burning here huh?"

I held my tongue.

"No honey, it's okay I just wanted to reach out to her again to see if there was something else we could do but I'll just dial the number again and see what happens. You can go now, and don't worry."

Cate turned on her spiked heels and headed back to her desk. Either she was an Oscar winning actress or she didn't have a clue. I'm betting on the latter. And that in itself left me even more confused. I thought for a quick minute and decided to call the number on the sticky-note again. This time I would leave a message. Not just any message. I wanted to leave one that would make Serena, whoever she was, want to call me back. I had to put on an Oscar gown of my own. I dialed the number. Voice mail again.

"Hey Serena! It has been forever, girl," I chirped. "I would love to get together for drinks on me. Say tomorrow after work? Maybe The Houndstooth on campus? Can't wait sweetie! Call me back!"

I hung up quickly and let out a huge breath. I purposely didn't leave my name. I wanted her to be curious and call my number back. My caller ID showed my number only and not my name so I felt pretty sure she'd call back. The thing was, I wasn't quite sure what I'd say when she did.

* * *

I waited for Annie in the lobby. Cate was in the downstairs powder room. I was nervous and fidgety. Not good for me. My plans were moving along between seeing Greg the next night and tracking down whoever this Serena was. My tightly wound world felt like it was coming undone again. I liked the predictability of my life before all of this. And it was making me super uncomfortable that Cate was coming on this little jaunt with Annie and me. I wouldn't be free to tell Annie my real thoughts.

"Alrighty Abby, let's go," Annie announced as she entered the foyer. "You ready?"

"Yep, just waitin' on Cate." I popped my eyebrows up.

"Oh, well I have a little idea." Annie moved closer to me and whispered, "Why don't we just go to the Battle- Friedman place first then we can tell her we aren't coming back to work today and run over to DePalma's and grab a bite to eat? It'll be a late lunch but we have so much to talk about."

"Great idea. I need to get you all caught up and that's perfect," I agreed.

Cate came out of the little powder room just behind the massive front staircase and joined us. "I'm ready if y'all are. Whose car are we takin'?"

Annie and I looked at each other. I jumped in. "Just go ahead and take your car. Annie and I have one more errand for a commercial she's doing and we won't be coming right back here. So just follow us then you can come back after we finish up at the venue."

"Oh, okay, I guess I'll just pick up some lunch on the way back." Cate looked disappointed.

"Yes but I promise maybe we can all do lunch together tomorrow," Annie broke in, ever the sweet-hearted softie.

"Sure," I gave in. "Great idea." Even though it wasn't. I smiled at them both and we made our way to the parking lot, Annie and I in my car, and Cate in her little light blue VW bug. She was only a couple of years younger than me but she was much less mature. Though she and Colleen were twins like Annie and me, Colleen had been much more successful at her career. They had both tested their chops in TV news and neither of them did so well. Cate was better on the air than her sister but Colleen always had the better grades in our marketing classes. Cate was newer at this side of the business. Though I originally thought she might be spying and helping Greg, I now thought she was just trying to do a good job. One thing was certain; she didn't seem to know a thing about Serena. If she had she would have put a name on the sticky note knowing I would have to call that person. Plus she wouldn't be going with us, knowing her note and that number were both fake. Surely we were fixin' to confirm that when we got to the venue. I knew Cate would never come along and be faced with that lie right in front of her when Jeanette who booked the place would swear up and down that she never called me this week. So I knew Cate was in the clear—at least when it came to that note and Serena, whoever that was, who had called and pretended to cancel my booking.

Whoever Serena was, she was in it without Cate. And as far as Cate goes, I almost actually liked her. At least for that day.

CHAPTER TWENTY

We walked the grounds of the historic Battle- Friedman Home. The afternoon was warm and breezy, typical spring afternoon in the Deep South. The fragrance of azaleas and magnolias was a heady concoction of sweet perfume and lush greens. The blue skies were cloudless and the camellia bushes dotted with rosy pink petals that surrounded the wide front porch welcomed us inside. It was so serene just being in the gardens of this enchanting historic place.

I remember coming here as a child for tours when I was in grade school. Even then I knew this place held magic. It felt like I had disappeared into another time and place. The entrance was so large and welcoming and the ceilings were over 10 feet high and carved with plaster designs and ornamentation. The Battle-Friedman House was built about 1835 by Alfred Battle, a North Carolina native who had come to Tuscaloosa in 1821. The house and its outbuildings occupied the entire city block. The grounds themselves were something to behold, with so many magnolia trees and a large gazebo. The columned porch and the rooms at the back of the house were added at various times before the Civil War. In 1875, Bernard Friedman, a local merchant who had emigrated from Hungary, bought the house from the Battles. It remained in the

Friedman family until 1965, when Hugo Friedman willed it to the city of Tuscaloosa. The burnt orange exterior of the house is stucco over brick and painted to resemble red marble. It is eye-catchingly stunning. The front porch has gorgeous paneled square columns, which is distinctively Tuscaloosa, as unusual as the city itself. Inside, elaborate plasterwork decorates the walls and ceilings of the front parlors and hallways. The richly decorated home was filled with renaissance revival furniture. I loved it so much there. I was suddenly so thankful the event would be held here. It was the perfect spot. It was far and away my favorite among the old historic homes of Tuscaloosa. I was so proud we had snagged it for the Mother's Day event and it had all worked itself out.

We walked into the grand entrance admiring the period details of the pre-Civil War pieces and artifacts that were scattered throughout. Jeanette was waiting for us at the scheduling desk. She was a petit lady with dark blonde hair. She wore a pale yellow sweater with small pink flowers and a string of pearls at her neckline. Little glasses sat perched on her nose, accented by a wide smile when she saw us enter. Jeanette was about 10 years older than Annie and me but we had known her all our lives. Our mother's were acquainted in the local social clubs when we were growing up.

"Hey honey, so good to see you," Annie cooed as we approached.

"And you too!" Jeanette popped as she stood up to give Annie a hug. That's the official greeting of the Deep South; hugs.

"How in the world are y'all? I haven't seen you two in foreveh." Jeanette said as she leaned over and hugged me next.

"We're good. Just working away," I answered. "So excited to get this perfect place for our Mother's Day event."

"Yes well I am so happy that poor lady cancelled. I mean not that she had to cancel her wedding but you know, nobody would be happy about a cancelled wedding, but oh, you know what I mean." Jeanette was gabby and never quite knew just what to say. It was one of the traits that made her so endearing.

"Let me show y'all all around." She continued to move from behind her desk as she glanced over at Cate.

"Oh, forgive me," I interrupted, "let me introduce my new assistant PR director, Cate Cantrell." They greeted each other as I watched closely. Cate seemed impervious. Nothing. So Annie stepped back and allowed me to follow Jeanette through the house. I told Cate to take pictures but we were only going to use the grand foyer and dining areas inside. The event would mostly be outside. As we walked around the home I decided I needed to put it all out there since I had been told by a supposed representative that the place wasn't available.

"Jeanette, I was just wondering, does anyone named Serena work here?"

"No, I have been here for so many years now and we never had anyone work here by that name. Why do you ask?"

"I had a woman by that name call me and tell me that there had been a mistake and that the place was booked after-all on Mother's Day."

"Now why in the world would anyone ever do a thing like that?" She plundered "That just simply make no sense at all."

"I know it. But I did speak to her myself. She had left a message for me and the conversation was about this home so there was no mistake. Someone didn't want us here that day."

"That is just totally weird," she surmised. "It certainly wasn't me or any of the staff here. Are you certain that was her name?"

"Oh yes. I even called the number back today—twice—and that is her name. I was as confused as you seem to be," I agreed.

Just then my phone rang. I pulled it from my purse and studied the number. "Speak of the devil. This is that Serena calling me back."

"Oh Lord, this should be very interesting," Annie chided.

"Oh I just can't believe it," Jeanette added.

"Let me take it. I'll be right back," I promised as I walked away for privacy. Mainly so Jeanette wouldn't hear the scam I was pulling. I walked out to the front porch from the front hall and stepped to the side pausing to think before I answered. I knew she would have no idea who was calling her. My number was obviously unrecognizable, and then I realized I would have no idea who to say I was. I didn't even have any idea who *she* was! I had to think. My heart raced as the phone kept ringing, urgently. What to do—oh dear I didn't want to miss her call. She would get my voicemail and hear my name. Oh Lord. I hit the answer button and tried to make myself sound chirpy and like I knew her. *Here goes*, I thought.

"Hey Serena girl, how in the world are yew?" I thickened my already southern lilt.

"Oh honey, is this Diane? I thought that was you. You got yourself a new phone number but I'd know that voice anywhere!"

Score!

"Yeah girl this is Diane. How 'bout those drinks? The Houndstooth? Say 5?"

I knew I told Ben I would see him and this would at least give me a chance to find out who this Serena was. My heart thumped in my throat.

"You got it girl. It's been forever. See you then!"

"Cain't wait," I pushed. I hung up before I *threw* up! This was so unlike me. I had never done anything like this. And honestly, I wasn't sure how or even *if* I could pull it off. But five o'clock was coming and I had a date with some little snake named Serena!

CHAPTER TWENTY-ONE

"My Lord, Abby, how in the world are you gonna handle this? I mean I'm sure you've thought of this but you don't even know what this girl looks like. You don't have her last name or we could look her up on Facebook. What are you gonna do?" Annie was visibly upset now that I deeply into this lie, uhm, predicament. I had actually talked to the girl and made plans to meet her—as Diane. What had I done?

Annie and I had finished up at the Battle-Friedman Home, said goodbye to Cate and we were sitting in the front bar area of DePalma's waiting for a table. The Art Deco front with the black and white striped awnings over the avocado glass paneled French doors welcomed us inside. It was such a cute spot. Both of us were sipping mimosas and chatting on the couch in front of the massive window to the right of the front doors, quietly just in case anyone we might know happened to be nearby. The rustic little room just inside the Italian restaurant was upscale casual with floor to ceiling windows and a gorgeous sweeping bar. I had suddenly lost my appetite and wanted nothing but drinks. Annie ordered appetizers and we stayed put on the soft overstuffed white couch in the little cozy room. I knew I was getting in knee deep and I was pretty nervous.

"I have no idea what I'm gonna do. I mean I have to go. This woman is obviously trying to connive to mess things up for me and for the station. I think this is actually part of my job," I explained.

"I agree," Annie said, "but listen—if you go in there and can't pull this off it could be the undoing of the whole thing. You'll never get to the bottom of this and find out who's behind it all."

"Well what the hell am I gonna do?" I panicked. "I mean I am very obviously not Diane. And, I don't not know what she looks like. Come to think of it, I have no idea at all how to even spot her when I get there. Oh Annie what have I done? I am such an idiot."

"No, no stop this—I will help you figure this whole thing out. This is my area, not yours. I'm coming with you and I will surely be able to help –somehow." Annie took a swig, throwing her head back to get the last drop of her drink, then looked up at the clock. "It's almost time. I think I have an idea that might work. Let's go." She had a steely look of determination on her face. She sat her drink down and threw one last bite of calamari into her mouth before getting up and giving me a stern look. "We can do this, and we must. C'mon."

I actually felt more nervous now than I did before. Annie could blow this whole thing and I was totally focused to get to the bottom of it. I felt the alcohol swirl in my head as I got up. And I had made a drink date with some girl named Serena. I certainly didn't need one more drink, the two, or was it three were enough for now. I had to remember I was meeting Ben at his house in just over an hour. "Oh, God, Annie, this is a disaster in the making," I said moving toward the door.

"Abby stop this obsessing, you're making me nervous. Now stand up straight and follow me. My Lord, you barely had more than two drinks. You never could hold your alcohol; you're such a lightweight. What am I gonna do with you if you are falling down drunk in front of this unknown woman. It will be all up to me. Please pull it together," she bossed.

Annie was walking faster than me as we headed to the car. She would have to drive. That was a no-brainer. But the drinks actually were making my head a little spinny.

The Houndstooth wasn't too far, just down the strip headed back toward campus. It had a huge outdoor patio and a nice big bar inside. It was usually loud but since it wasn't football season, maybe I could actually hear what Serena would be saying, that was if this ringing in my ears would just stop. Annie found a close spot across the little boulevard and down the side street near the Waffle House—which surely would be an answer to prayer after more drinks. Annie and I hurried across the street and onto the outdoor patio. Annie stopped in her tracks once we arrived and gazed around like she had any clue what she might be searching for.

"Okay, I give," I said, "How do you plan to find her? In case you've forgotten, we don't really know what the hell she looks like because we don't know her!" I popped my eyebrows up, still a little unsteady.

"Look," Annie popped, "either you trust me or you don't. Just follow my lead."

That totally scared me.

It was five o'clock straight up and down and the work crowd was shuffling in. "Just look for a woman alone, about our age. There can't be too many to fit that bill if you think about it."

Sounded like it might work—okay I'll go with it.

"And look—if we see someone that might be her, I know just what to do," Annie bragged.

Oh God, I wanted to squint my eyes and miss the wreck but I kept peeking and crossing my fingers.

"Okay there's a lady, that short brunette that just passed us. She's inside now at the bar. Just let me do all the talking."

Annie if you do and it's actually her…" I tried but she was heading inside at a clip.

"Watch this." She said over her shoulder.

I wanted to scream nooooooo, but it was too late.

"Serena! Is that you?"

Oh. My. God.

The woman turned and scowled at us. Clearly not Serena.

"I beg your pardon," the brunette says.

"Oh, honey I am so sorry, I thought you were someone else." Annie oozed. *Okay*, I thought, *she's pretty good.*

"Okay who shall we frighten next?" I said dripping with sarcasm followed by an evil smile.

"Stop it, Abby. You have to admit this is a good idea. There's another lonely lady, and she's obviously looking for someone. I can tell."

Uh huh. I felt like we were lesbian lovers looking for our next threesome, using old pick up lines but I fell in right behind Annie so she could lead me to Serena. I had to know just what was going on with her and why she would try to wreck my event. I had to stay focused.

"Serena! So great to see you!" The curvy blue-eyed lady turned.

"Do I know you? Yes, it's Diane silly. Meet my sister, Donna. So great to see you!"

"That is so funny, I do plan to meet my friend here and her name is Diane but I know you're not her. Isn't that a hoot?"

"Oh C'mon, it's me silly. I've just had a little work done. You know the boobs, the hair, even had a nose job but it's me, in the flesh."

Annie was certainly kin to Mother. She could act and improve like a pro.

"Come sit over here and let's get all caught up! I'll have whatever she's having. Make that two –one for my sister," Annie said to the bartender. Annie turned back to a stunned Serena.

"You look amazing!" Serena said studying Annie—ala, Diane, in her newly changed state of appearance.

Then Annie led us both to a table in the back, a darkened little corner so it wouldn't be so obvious that she wasn't Diane.

Dark was what we needed for sure. Annie's confidence had taken over. We all sat down at the small table and Annie leaned in for more.

"So tell me what all have you been up to? How long's it been since I saw you?"

"Uhm, Uhm, well it has been a few months," Serena stumbled. "I just cannot get over your transformation! It's unreal."

"Yeah I know, pretty great huh? Anyhoo, catch me up honey, are you seeing anyone?"

I took a long swig of my margarita. We all had one, salty and on the rocks. I kept licking the salt trying to get something in my stomach so it would absorb the alcohol. I totally knew that line of thinking was heavily flawed.

"Oh, well a couple of new guys have cropped up here lately. But one of them's a real cutie pie. You might know him. He works in radio I think. I just met him, oh what are the call letters of that thing? Oh yeah WRBI."

I accidentally sniffed the salt up my nose as I choked on the lime. I had to hear her say his name. It couldn't be—could it? Annie glanced at me and popped an eyebrow. She smiled and said, "Oh my, you're right. I do probably know him, you know, small town. Who is it?"

"Oh I shouldn't say anything this early, but he may be meeting me here after he gets off." She took a swig and stirred her drink with a grin. I was totally losing it. It better not be who I thought she might be talking about. I needed my information and I was fixin' to blurt it out when Annie did it for me.

"Honey, I heard recently that you had made a call to this woman I used to know. I really can't stand her but I heard from a mutual friend that you made a call to that woman at WRCT— Abby Harper. She said you were told to tell her the Battle Friedman Home was overbooked. Girl that was a good one! Who told you to do that? That is just brilliant!"

"What? Who could have told you that? I was helping someone, that's all. I wanna know who told you, that was private."

Just then as I was dizzy and starting to swell from all the salt, "Hey Serena! How do you know Abby and Annie?" Greg Galloway stood towering over Serena's chair.

CHAPTER TWENTY-TWO

"Abby and Annie?" Serena popped. "No, this is Diane and Donna." Annie grabbed my hand and yanked me up and ran out the door through the outdoor patio and across the street to the car, dragging me behind her all the way. I was dizzy and my head was churning with what had just happened. Annie clicked the doors open as we approached the car and we both jumped inside. I could barely catch my breath.

"Oh no, Annie, this is not good. Now Greg will know. She will tell him and I have plans with him tomorrow night."

"You what? You left that part out when you were catching me up at DePalma's. Why in the world are you seeing him? What about Ben?"

"I was going to flirt with him and maybe he would let something slip," I explained.

"Yes, I am quite sure he would let something slip—and I know you know just what he'd want to slip and where he'd want to slip it. This is crazy. She was obviously put up to this by someone and now we can make a accurate assumption as to just who is behind all this—it's Greg Galloway—still up to his old tricks. That guy is such a sleeze!"

"No," I yelped, "I just still cannot believe he would want to ruin me. He always had to be on top. Maybe it's Colleen.

Maybe she's friends with Serena and she is trying to impress Greg," I reasoned.

"No matter what, it's all coming from that station. And I wouldn't trust him for a minute. Dinner? Abby you have officially lost your mind. Ben is waiting. I need to get you back to the station so you can meet him. Why don't we call him to meet us there so he can drive you?"

"Okay, I'll call him now," I said. I somehow felt defeated. Was it Colleen or Greg? I guess it really didn't matter. At this point Annie was right—it was all coming from the same place so it really *didn't* matter. I just wanted to see Ben. This day had been draining and I was craving an evening with him. I glanced up and the bright yellow Waffle House sign was buzzing overhead. I knew just what I wanted. Biscuits and redeye gravy. That would be the perfect cure for all this spinning my head was doing. Looks like dinner would be right here. I called Ben and told him to meet me there.

"I'm gonna leave when he gets here and I know you're in good hands," Annie said.

"How is it that you're now the mother? This is usually my role," I said in my still dizzy state.

"Abby, we take care of each other. We always have. You just don't like the loss of control but you have a lot going on right now and I'm here. Know that. You have to let those who love you help you when you need it. Okay?"

I smiled at her and laid my head on her shoulder. She was right. We had always been just like this. Annie and I had a bond like no other. And it wasn't just because we were twins. People have always said that. Twins are always close but Annie and I were different and I knew why. We were not only twins but we had a shared history of living with the woman we called Mother. Toots Harper Cartwright, as she is known by her friends, was indeed a strange mix of both nurture and insanity. She was secretive yet loud, loyal yet sneaky. And she raised us in a home full of those secrets and her embarrassingly bad behavior. Annie always knew what was going on but she tried to smile right through it. She was compliant. Malleable. I also knew what was going on with our mother but I was much more verbal and pushy. I wanted Mother to stop sneaking around. Oh we never knew whom it was she was seeing until last year, but we all knew she was seeing a man and never was down at the Gulf with her girlfriends.

All the while, Daddy had his head buried in the sand. I believe he must have known too but wouldn't allow himself to really believe it, that his tall leggy brunette beauty queen would be seeing another man. His very own brother! He would have sworn on a stack of bibles she was devoted to him—and to us. But Mother was wired differently. She had a confidence like I had never seen and so she would do her own thing without batting a false eyelash. She could and did compartmentalize her life. At home she was our Mother until about 11pm, then she was out the back door, tip-toeing across the tile in the kitchen as the back door slowly clicked shut behind her. I would cry myself to sleep—facing Annie in the bed next to me, tears falling down her cheeks, she would gaze at me and offer a child-like smile and turn over to face the wall.

We thought we must be the only kids in the world with a mother like ours. We held each other up and kept each other laughing.

My older sister Rhonda was more aggressive and would fight with Mother when she denied everything. Rhonda started spending more and more time out of the house to get away from all the secrets and lies.

So it was just Annie and me. Just like it was at that moment. Just like it always had been and always would be. It gave me comfort as we sat there under the buzzing bright yellow glow of the waffle House sign that night.

* * *

Ben came to the Waffle House and joined us in some high calorie delicious supper and we ate ourselves silly, my tummy full of biscuits and redeye gravy, hash browns and waffles. My nerves and anxiety satisfied. My head had stopped spinning. Annie had gone on to the home she now shared with Matt.

Ben and I drove through the quiet streets of Tuscaloosa making our way to his house nestled in an older section of town, under the old oaks and giant magnolias off University Boulevard. The evening was still and peaceful as we entered the Historic districts. The houses in this area were built in the early 20th Century. The Caplewood and Pinehurst historic neighborhoods sit like books on a shelf, one after the other in the old section of Tuscaloosa. Ben bought an old turn of the century Tudor style place that faced University Boulevard and backed up against the University Club at the top of the street just before it intersects with Queen City Avenue.

We pulled slowly into his long driveway going under a side porch until the car rolled to a stop.

"Here we are," he smiled. "Welcome to my humble abode." He leaned over and kissed my cheek. Yes, I was full and very satisfied.

"I can't wait to see the inside," I marveled. "I have passed this place a thousand times and it always stood out to me. The Tudor style and this side entrance—just so historic."

"Yeah, I bought this place a couple of years ago and just wait'll you see the inside. I have restored it as best I could. I even had a restoration expert here and we shined her up pretty good. I guess I just have a thing for old homes and history." Ben reached in from the open roof of his roadster and opened my door for me, extending his had for me to hold as I stepped out of his car.

"I want to take you in the front door for the grand effect, so follow me," he grinned like a kid on Christmas morning. We walked around to the front door—a little cove with an arched red door like it belonged to a little elf. It was just perfect. "Okay," he continued, "close your eyes."

I heard Ben unlock the door. It creaked as it swung open. I kept my eyes closed. Then he stepped behind me and covered my eyes. "Okay, you ready?"

"Yes, I can't wait," I giggled.

"Okay here's the masterpiece!" Ben slipped his soft hands away from my face to reveal a huge curved staircase, the banister following it up as it swept to the compelling upstairs landing. I had never seen anything like it. It was all plaster and wood as if floating upwards to heaven. The cobblestone foyer lead to the magnificent staircase and just underneath it was a little cove with another arched little door. This home was unlike anything I had ever been in and Ben had it so perfectly restored I felt like I was stepping back to the Belle Epoch in Europe. I was literally stunned. My mouth dropped open in pure awe.

"Oh my goodness, Ben! This is just beautiful! I don't even know what to say."

"So you like it?"

"I love it. I couldn't love it more. One of my little secret loves is historical homes and restoring them. I so wish I had been part of this. I just love all the details! It is truly remarkable."

"Good well I will take you on the grand 5-cent tour." Ben held out his arm and I crooked my arm in the bend of his as we headed toward the back. As we walked through the house I felt like I was seeing a deeper side of Ben, a side I don't think I ever knew—even when we were back in college. Ben showed me through the illustrious downstairs, the restored perfect kitchen with exposed brick, a chef's stove with red knobs and a pot filler and six burners. The dining hall was massive and perfectly restored with wainscoting and toile fabric wallpaper in red.

Ben then slipped his arm down and laced his fingers in mine as he led me up the curved floating staircase to the bedrooms. And then to his master's retreat. My heart quickened as we entered the masculine space. All done in pale robin's egg blues and deep browns, it had a serenity all its own. A white brick fireplace stood catty-cornered near the floor to ceiling French doors that lead to a Juliette balcony that faced the lush landscaped backyard, a garden of roses and camellias, hydrangeas and pink peonies.

I sat down on the side of the bed and gazed at the perfectly plastered ornate ceiling done in Wedgewood patterns. The attention to detail was just spectacular.

"So, you like what you see?" Ben teased.

"Oh yes, I certainly do sir," I played back. Ben stepped in front of me and positioned himself between my knees as I lay back onto his soft plush bedding. Ben lay across me and kissed me softly. Yes I knew I was fixin' to have a whole new definition of full and satisfied.

CHAPTER TWENTY-THREE

I loved feeling Ben's weight on me. He had gone over and lit the fireplace before he began kissing me so softly and gently, just brushing his lips against mine, tasting me, teasing me. I moved backwards so we would be across the center of the bed, Ben kept kissing me as we moved in unison. He pulled back, gazing at me.

"If you don't want this right now, just tell me. I don't want to push you, Abby. You mean too much to me and you've had a rough day. I understand," he reassured.

"Ben, does it look like I'm uncomfortable? I know we just got reacquainted but seriously, I know you're just what I need. Seriously I have missed you but I thought you'd never want to look at me again after the way things ended. I do want you. And Ben, I'm not a scared little twenty-two year old this time." I pushed my fingers through his thick dark hair and pulled him closer kissing him passionately. He pulled my blouse out of my pants and placed his hand on my abdomen, working his way up to my breasts. Cupping his long slender fingers over the lace I felt heat rise as I pulled his button-down from his pants and slipped my hand down the front and into his underwear wrapping my hand around his large manhood. He was large and protective and slow and deliberate—a fantasy of perfection.

The blue of the moon streamed through the sheer drapes and splashed all over the wood floor. The flames of the fireplace met it and the evening dance of moon-shadows and firelight began as Ben and I were in our own mesmerized ecstasy, a provocative striptease as I enjoyed each stage of exposure; both mine—and his. He twisted the buttons of my blouse and removed it completely, my bra unhooked from the front and Ben wasted no time in unfastening it and exposing my round breasts to him. He stopped to look at me and smiled. "You are the same yet so different," he crooned. "I want you, Abby."

"You can have me anytime Ben."

Ben caressed my breasts maddeningly slowly as he straddled me, kneading my flesh. He leaned down and licked my nipple swirling his tongue around the edges and sucking the tip into his mouth. My hands wandered around to his backside and cupped his butt, squeezing his ass while I felt his tongue enter my lips. His hands moved to my pants and I helped him arching my back upwards into his hard cock, he slipped them off along with my panties in one move. I was fully naked underneath him. The full nudity felt cool on my skin though I was on fire inside.

"You are so beautiful," Ben whispered as he pulled back to see me stretched out beneath him fully exposed. I smiled and caressed his hips. He removed his shirt and I felt him wriggle out of his pants. Both of us now fully exposed and naked in front of each other for the first time in so many years. We were man and woman now, not two college kids and it felt more real. I was filled with desire and heat as Ben moved himself between my thighs. I allowed him to, wrapping my legs around his perfect buttocks, as Ben positioned himself to enter me. He slid one hand under the small of my back and lifted me up to meet him. I felt him enter me with a thrust. I inhaled with a ragged breath as he closed his eyes. The sensation of having him inside me and the emotions playing out on his face were almost too much to bear. I wanted him more than I ever had. I wanted more of this, more of us. I wanted him to come undone and know that I had done this; that we had done this together and it was so long waiting to have Ben back—something I never thought would happen.

We found our own perfect rhythm as he moved in and out me in a cadence of passion. My hands slipped down the tensing muscles of his back feeling his pace quicken, his breath become more labored. I felt the curve of his butt fill my hands as I arched upwards to take more of him inside. He was deliberate and careful, so considerate yet filled with masculine hungry passion. I had never had feelings like this making love to either him or Greg in my past. It felt deep and real and in a far away place of my heart that had never been touched before. Maybe I had never let anyone in that spot before. I saw Ben's pleasure on his perfectly chiseled face, wrenched in erotic desire; his eyes squinted under his furrowed brow, his teeth clamped down on his bottom lip. We erupted together in one motion, I kept my eyes open so I could watch Ben making love to me, his passion exploding, he looked down at me before he finished, as if I were the only woman on earth.

He collapsed on me, his breath measured and rapid on my skin, his face nestled between my breasts, I had never felt this way—literally one with someone else. Of all the time we had made love in college I had never felt this close to Ben. I had never let anyone this close to me. It was different now because I was finally ready. This was real. It was deep and overwhelming. I began to feel the sting of salty tear fill my eyes. Ben noticed.

"Abby, are you okay. Did I hurt you? Were you not ready?" His concern for me was so genuine. I don't think I had ever felt that either. At least I was probably too self-absorbed to notice it.

"Oh Ben, I'm just overwhelmed. I mean I care for you so much, maybe more than I was ready to admit. I've missed you but we are so different now."

"I hope so," he answered, "but in a good way right?"

I giggled as I ran my fingers through his hair. He was still lying on my chest breathing rapidly and caressing my abdomen, drawing swirls along my skin with his fingers.

"Of course, in a wonderful way. Ben this is the most wonderful and satisfied I have ever felt and it's not because you made love to me like this—it's because I felt so close to you."

"I know babe, it was different for me too. I felt like we were one. Like we were in sync, you know, well in many ways we were," he grinned and reached upwards kissing my cheek.

We lay there for at least an hour caressing and feeling each other's flesh. It was a quiet time of satisfaction and such peace as the firelight danced on the ornate ceiling. Ben's room was cool and the hum of the evening played like a symphony outside, evening doves and crickets in a rhythm of their own, the leaves rustled in the warm breeze as the curtains fluttered. The fragrant blossoms mixed with the aroma of freshly mown yards created a heady concoction of perfume. I was in such a place of relaxation I felt I was floating. Like nothing mattered anymore. Just Ben and me. Alone in our own shared little universe. Then Ben broke the spell.

"Abby, I need to tell you something. It's important. I have wanted to tell you this for the last week but I thought it might scare you away."

I felt instantly nervous. My heart sped up and I felt a tightness spread across my body, tensing up and getting ready for the blow. I swallowed hard as I turned to Ben who was now propped up on his elbow. I braced myself.

"Abby, please understand, I know this is sudden and you are surely not ready." He was the one now swallowing hard. He looked anxious, uncomfortable. I wondered why he wanted to do this now. Just moments ago we were in our own little paradise, loving and tasting and enjoying each other. What could he have to say and why say it now?

"Okay. I'm ready," I said bristling. "Is it awful? Is there

someone else and you want to go back to her? Tell me, I pleaded; I'm fixin' to die here Ben. This is obviously very important and I need..."

Ben placed his index finger over my chattering lips. "I love you, Abby." He grinned. "I never stopped. I can't. You are a part of me. You always have been and I have never figured out what I should do with these feelings. Even when I was with Colleen, I could never stop thinking of you. I love you. I do." He stopped abruptly and gazed at me. "That was it. That was what I had to say."

I felt my stomach drop and an uncontrollable smile crept across my face. Ben was still naked, lying next to me, all man and muscle and dark thick hair, but he was so cute and innocent and genuine. In that moment, I knew I loved him too, more than I ever had. We were meant to be together. I felt secure in that.

I reached over and ran my fingers through his mass of dark waves. "I love you too, Ben. I do. I never stopped either. I couldn't. You were always part of me too and I have known forever that you always would be." I smiled at him as he leaned over and kissed me slowly, his fingers tangled in my hair as he dropped his hand around the back of my neck and pulled me closer.

I rolled over and straddled him as we kissed and wandered and felt each other's body. I pulled back and gazed into his deep blue eyes. He smiled back at me was beautiful. A perfect man in every way. I suddenly felt playful and remembered he was ticklish just under his ribs. I began and he laughed a deep rolling laugh that I had always loved. He rolled me over and I felt his fingers under my jaw. "Hey that's not fair, I was working on you," I laughed.

"This is the spot," he laughed back at me. "I could never forget." He tickled my neck and as I always had, I would laugh until I lost my breath. I sounded like the cat Sylvester trying to say 'sufferin' succotash.' We tickled and giggled until I was out of breath. I jumped up and gathered my clothes, running into the master bath. "I'm getting dressed. We both have to work in the morning," I said.

"You can stay here," he offered. "I will get up early and take you home so you can get ready for work. Sound good?"

I had to think about it—for like a split second.

"Okay," I yelled back. "I'll be right out. Do you have a shirt I can sleep in?"

"Of course I do, I mean if you really need it," he chortled.

His bathroom was spectacular, all done in period sconce lighting and hexagon tiles. A magnificent claw foot tub stretched out in the corner and the pale grayish blue walls glowed in the perfect amber lighting. I went to the sink and put my clothes down on the smooth marble vanity. I caught myself in the mirror and I had to take a moment. *Could this really be happening?* I wondered. How strange and exciting it suddenly felt. Ben Flannigan. Wow. He was back in my life and had just told me he loved me. And I was so sure I loved him too. All that frenetic wound-up tight energy of my past began to let loose, unwind. I felt like I could breathe, like everything would be okay.

I twisted the vintage knob of the sink and cool water poured out. I cupped my hand beneath the flow and splashed my face. Peace. I felt peace. Then I heard my phone buzz in my pants pocket—a text.

"Hey, good running into you tonight. We still on for our date tomorrow night?" I glanced up at the name—Greg Galloway.

CHAPTER TWENTY-FOUR

The cool of the morning hung in the quiet mist as Ben drove me to get my car. It was nearly sunrise and I had to get my car from the station, get home for a quick shower and get dressed for work. The Warrior River was always shrouded in a thin veil of mist in the Alabama springtime. Ben lived so near the river. It made everything damp and cool and fragrant. The early mornings were like a private sanctuary, all before the hustle bustle of the day begins, the peace and solitude were like a much-needed sedative, or a tall glass of water after a day in the blistering sun. It made me feel connected to my own soul.

The drive with Ben was quiet. Both of us were in a place deep within ourselves. I knew at least for me I was reliving the seductive events of last night and all that it meant. The new place I was in with Ben felt so good, and so real. I felt stronger about him now than I did in college and that was a strange feeling. We were different people now, and we fit together better. Maybe it was just me. Ben was always the old soul and really he hadn't changed all that much. He was still very old-fashioned and chivalrous, and he still treated me like a princess. I suppose it took me all these years to catch up to him. I was a little immature if I recall. Back then anyway.

Ben drove to the back lot and pulled in next to my car. The

rays of first light were just peeking in from the eastern edge of town.

"I hope you rested well," he said leaning over to kiss me.

"I did. It was the most peaceful comfortable night I've had in forever. Thank you," I oozed kissing him softly back. And it had been the perfect night. I didn't want it to end.

"I loved waking up next to you. I will always love that," he smiled.

"Me too. It felt really good," I said.

"So, tonight? Are you busy?" Ben asked innocently.

But I wasn't so innocent. I knew I had agreed to see Greg. It was only for me to see if I could sense anything from him. And now I had even more on the line, ever since I met Serena at Houndstooth the night before. I knew he had something sneaky going on and I thought he might let something slip. I also knew I had to be careful. I didn't want to lead him on so he would go over the edge, but I believed if I could lead him just far enough he would let the cat out of the bag before he even knew it. At least I hoped. The thing was Ben didn't know. And I knew he would feel uneasy if he did.

Ben and I had just gotten to this new place, and both of us had just said I love you. I most surely didn't want to mess that up by telling Ben now that I was seeing Greg to try to trick him out of some secret information about the Mother's Day event. I didn't want to taint what had just happened between Ben and me so I kept silent about my plans with Greg. I lied.

"I do have plans," I said cringing at my fib. "I have something to do with my Book Club. I wish I could get out of it but I made this commitment a while back. But I will call you when it's over." I grinned at him and consciously promised myself that I would end the night early and come straight home. I kissed Ben one last time and got out of his car. I watched him watching me as I made my way to my car and got in. I backed out and drove past him, blowing a kiss as I did and turned out onto 15th Street and headed home.

This little white lie made me nervous. I had a bad feeling

in the pit of my stomach about the whole thing. About seeing Greg and what he might try but mostly about not telling Ben the truth. It gnawed away at me as I drove home.

I pulled into my drive and saw the azaleas still scattered on my porch. Anger rose inside of me and I felt the serenity of the morning evaporate like the mist hovering above the inky river. I got out and stepped over the dying flowers to see a note attached to my front door. Mitzy strikes again. I barely cared what she had to say except for the small fact that my doorknob was missing. I opened the note as I pushed through my front door.

Dear Ms. Harper.

Well, well, aren't we the smart one? You think you can just talk your way out of an arrest. Well guess what? I saw your man outside my house after midnight the other night and I was able to get a decent picture of him as he replanted my mailbox. I plan to turn this into the police if you don't stop with all of these demands to fix the shared ally-way. Now whose ball is in whose court Ms. Harper? I though you'd see things my way. I know you wouldn't want your new lover arrested and in trouble with the law. And speaking of said lover, please for the love of God, don't have your little sex parties in front of your windows and outdoors in the middle of the night. I heard all that talking and laughing coming from your backyard. As a life coach, I must follow my own advice and get my ten hours of sleep. All that "entertaining" has messed up Al Roker's schedule too. Believe me, you don't want to run into him when he is exhausted and you and your man are having too much to drink. He has not been declawed.

I will expect new plants I can tolerate in the shared alley-way by tomorrow evening, say boxwoods or another non-flowering shrub. If not, your lover's picture will be with the Tuscaloosa Police Department in 48 hours. I may even turn it into the newspaper. Think about it, Ms. Harper. But then again, you seem like the type who might like those rough types.

Mitzy Montgomery

I was fuming so badly. I went straight out back to the garage and grabbed my can of hot pink spray paint and marched right to her porch. It was barely light outside so I wouldn't be seen, not that I even thought about that as I moved like I was race-walking right to her house. Before I could stop myself I had painted a directive on her porch I knew I would later regret, BITE ME in big letters stared me back in the face. I ran like hell to my back door and went inside before anyone would notice me. I was officially losing it. I hurried upstairs and got in the shower. My heart was still racing about the deed I had just committed—vandalism. I knew I needed to get away. I felt my life unraveling again just after the most dreamy magnificent night with Ben. All those years of total control and holding in my feelings was finally back-firing and I knew in that second that no matter how many nights I spent with Ben I needed to get away. I hadn't taken a vacation from work in two years. Everything was happening all at once and it obviously lay just under the surface. Any little bit of anger and pop, my head would nearly explode. It was like trying to close an over-stuffed trunk, things seeping out of every corner as I tried in vain to keep it all inside. No sooner had I gotten one side stuffed in and closed than the other end had more things falling out.

I stepped out of my shower. It was actually painful to leave my warm oasis. I knew I needed to get dressed in a hurry and get to work before Mitzy saw my new message and had the cops over again. I flew around the house like it was on fire. Hair, make-up and a granola bar in my hand, I hauled ass straight out to my car, jumped in and sped to work. I called my gardener, James, and asked him to hurry over and save those azaleas, telling him exactly where to plant them. I was trying desperately to regain some control, some composure. And I knew just what I had to do. Stay calm, get to the bottom of the event issues, and make sure I didn't screw it all up. Certainly I could keep it together just a little bit longer.

I slipped quietly into my office. Almost no one was there it was so early. Just the receptionist downstairs. Cate wasn't due in for another half hour and I was happy just for the moment alone. I could gather my thoughts, write my lists and take a much-needed deep breath. I walked into the upstairs coffee nook and made myself a fresh cup and walked back to my office. The warm liquid felt good and I savored it sipping slowly as I went through my emails, trying to catch up. Jeanette from the Battle-Friedman Home saying we are all set for the big Mother's day event. That was good—a confirmation and something positive. I had my huge Lilly Pulitzer planner open on my desk so I could see things at a glance and I took out my green pen and scribbled *confirmed* over the date, May 8th 2016. That was Mother's Day. I was feeling more in control already. Lists. They always made me feel better.

I leaned down and grabbed my purse so I could check my phone messages when I saw it. A note in my purse I didn't recognize. I opened the pale pink paper. Oh God, here we go again.

Dear Ms. Harper,
I know you are confused but just know I've got this. You can count on me. You will know who I am in due time but for now, I am handling the things that are bringing you down. Take care of yourself, especially when it comes to matters of the heart.
Sincerely,
Secret Sister

I leaned back in my desk chair. My heart quickened and my stomach dropped in shock. I suddenly felt even less secure and less in control. This certainly didn't help me relax. It made me totally uneasy. Who was this secret sister? I felt naked, like someone was watching me, spying on me. It made my skin prickle. I felt a shiver shoot down my spine. And what the hell does she mean, *matters of the heart*? Did she know about Ben?

How could she unless she was spying on me 24/7— I had to get up and walk around. And think. I stayed focused on the note itself and what it said, then the *who could it be* thoughts crept in. Then possibly the most important question blared like a megaphone in my head— *how the hell did that note get into my purse?*

I started going back through all the places I had been, from the event venue, to Houndstooths to Ben's house—everywhere I had stepped foot in the last twenty-four hours. Every single person I had run into and had any contact with came into my mind as I searched my memory and picked apart every single person. I had no clue.

I started cleaning my office, dusting and straightening my desk. Clean-freak.

It would be dumb for Annie to be pulling this, I thought to myself, so who knows? It could literally be anyone. I had seen waiters and waitresses and Jeanette and even folks at the Waffle House. There would be no way for me to figure this out. I had to tell Annie, I promised myself. I had to show her the two notes I had gotten so far from Secret Sister. Maybe she could help me piece this puzzle together.

I sat back down at my desk and took the other note out and re-read it, then put them both into a small white envelope and marked it S.S. for secret sister. I like to have everything labeled and filed and organized. I wiped my desk clean with a Kleenex and instantly felt better. A clean space. I took my cell phone out of my purse to get back to the next thing on my list— answering my texts. I clicked on my text messages and there it was staring me in the face—that message from Greg Galloway. I still hadn't answered him from last night. I felt my stomach twist. I closed my eyes and shook my head to myself. How did I get into such a ridiculous mess? I knew what I had to do. I knew I needed a long vacation from my job and incidentally, my entire life, but I wasn't leaving the business without a fight—without finally exposing Greg Galloway for exactly who he had always been—a fraud. Someone who can't come up with an original idea all his own—he had never once been able to do that, always stealing my ideas ever since college marketing 101.

Hey Greg, sure we are still on—text me when you're ready and I'll meet you.

Okay. It was on. I planned to get as much as I could out of him. Once and for all I would outsmart Greg. And I couldn't wait. I took out my planner and made a list of what I would do to lead the conversation, all the questions I would ask. One major item stood out like a blaring spotlight on that little list— who the hell was Serena and why was she calling me pretending to be someone else? He should know since she said they were seeing each other. I looked at my list and felt better. My lists were my savior. I could refer to them and always feel in control. And if something didn't go as planned, well, I could always clean something—and I guess there's always Secret Sister. At this point, she may have things more under control than I do.

CHAPTER TWENTY-FIVE

"Good morning Ms. Harper! Did you have a good night?" Cate was certainly full of cheer.

"Yes I had a nice night and you?" I popped back with a smile.

"Oh you know, the same. A bowl of soup and my cat for bed company."

"I would have thought you were the type to have a big night out most of the time."

"Why? Do I come across as a party girl?"

"Oh not exactly, I guess it's just…"

"The way I look?" Cate was intuitive. "I know. I get that a lot—you know, a body for sin type of thing. But really this body is just a home-body."

I could hear Cate getting situated at her desk. I still didn't fully trust her but I was starting to like her a little better. Just then Toni Lyn, the station manger appeared at my door.

"Hey how'd it go over at the Battle-Friedman Home yesterday? I never got those pictures you promised. Can you shoot me those ASAP?"

"Oh I'm sorry, sure. Right away," I retorted. I had surely forgotten as I was in Ben's arms not caring one bit about Toni Lyn Tingle for the entire night. But I knew I had to get her the lay of the land for the event. She smiled and shut the door moving closer to my desk.

"How's it going with Cate? I mean her time here is almost up and we need to send another candidate in."

"You know, I like her—actually more than I thought I would. I'd like her to stay on another week so I can try to get to know her a bit better."

"You got it," Toni Lyn agreed. "I'll talk with her this afternoon. Glad you like her."

"Well, I just feel like a week is barely enough time to know her abilities."

"You're the boss on this so whatever you'd like. I'll make the arrangements with the other candidates. I brought her in first because I thought she was the best of the candidates. Okay shoot me those pictures. Talk to you later." And with that she turned and opened the door and clicked her high heels down the back staircase. Her support made me feel good anyway. She was letting me decide what I wanted. Once I learned Cate didn't have anything to do with Serena and that fake call I felt better about her. I figured she was just working here to spy for her twin sister, Colleen. But maybe not. I promised myself I would try to get to know her better soon.

Just then Annie popped into my office.

"Hey girl so how was it?"

I motioned for her to shut the door.

"Sit down," I ordered with a smile on my face.

"Ooooh, I see. It was that good huh?" Annie said plopping down onto my floral couch near the massive window, a grin sweeping across her perfect little face.

"It was. Oh Annie, I can't believe I have another chance with Ben. He is too good. He is like a perfect man, a perfect gentleman and after the way it ended all those many years ago, after me embarrassing him in front of everyone we knew, he still loves me. Do I even deserve that?"

"Oh Abby, of course you do. But wait—did he say that? Did he actually tell you he loves you?"

I smiled at the recent memory. "He did. Just last night. And I said it back."

"Oh honey, I'm so happy for you."

"Last night was like no other time I have ever been with a man."

"If memory serves me correctly, you have actually only *been* with two men, the two that, to this day, still play a part in your life."

"Okay yes, thanks for the clarification, and the bleak reminder, but still, last night was different than it had ever been, even with Ben. We're both older—you know, in a different place now than all those years ago. It wasn't like just impassioned hungry sex. Ben made love to me. He looked into my eyes in the most heated moments, and told me he loved me. I felt like I was one with him. I never felt that before Annie—not ever."

"You should see that dreamy face of yours. Abby I love you and you so deserve this. Nothing matters more than feeling like you have a partner through thick and thin that will always have your back. That is what Matt does for me too. We are one. That's how it's s'posed to feel, honey."

"I just feel like things are spinning out of control you know?"

"Well, I surely know you need to have things clean and orderly. And since I saw you taking out your own garbage the other day, I knew things were out of order. So things have gotten worse? How?"

I took my little white envelope from my bag and handed it to Annie so she could see my notes from Secret Sister. Annie read them with her mouth dropped open.

"Oh my Lord, honey—what the hell?"

"I know. It's kinda creepy," I admitted.

"Any ideas just who it is?"

"Not one." I shook my head.

"Hmm, well lets look at the hand writing. I know it's print but there are some refined marks that could be telling. I don't recognize any of it but I know since it's in handwriting we can get to the bottom of it. It will take some work but we can do it." She handed me back the notes and I put them back in the white envelope.

"The strange thing is, someone is dropping them in my purse so it has to be someone who has access to it, and can get to it when I'm not looking."

That could be anyone we work with. Or any waitress – anyone. Anywhere.

"I know, it's driving me nuts, I added."

"Well you've got bigger fish to fry right? Like going out with Greg tonight. Any thoughts on what you might do and how you might get what you need from him?"

I pulled out my planner and pointed to my list smiling back at her.

"Of course, why am I not surprised? See you are not totally losing it—not yet. You have your list." Annie got up from the couch and walked over to my desk. I stood up as she approached, reaching out to give me a hug.

"It's all gonna be okay. You are still in control and I've got your back—and Ben's got your backside," she giggled. "Look, I'm serious. He loves you and you love him. This time it's the real grown-up love you've been longing for. Ben is wonderful. He always was. Let him in and let him be the man, Abby. He's really good at that, but you are so afraid to trust anyone else being in control of you. You have to loosen up and let him inside your life. I know it's what he wants. And truthfully I know it's what you want too. I love you. We got this—the whole thing. But most importantly, you have love— and really—what else do we need?"

Annie kissed my cheek and headed to my office door. She glanced over her shoulder and smiled as she turned the corner and headed down the stairs to prep for her show. I leaned back in my chair and thought about what she had said. It was all true. Annie certainly had found her calling, all we need is love, and she was a talk show host helping people find their lost loves. But the thing was, she was right. What else would or could matter if I had Ben's love? I had to learn to let go and let my life find itself. I hoped I could.

My mind began to wander. It stretched into the future at a possible life with Ben—the whole picture—kids and vacations and the whole happily ever after. I could actually see it. I had never been the one to believe in such things. Fairy tales were in Annie's neck of the woods. I was much more of a realist. I had carried the burdens my mother laid down and held Annie many nights as she cried herself to sleep not knowing where our Mother had gone in the middle of the night.

I glanced down at my planner and the date jolted me back to the moment—and the task at hand. The take-down of Greg Galloway, and my dreaded dinner date with him. Just then I got a text from Annie. She was downstairs in her studio.

"We promised Cate we'd take her to lunch. Still on?"

I had totally forgotten. But I knew that would be one way to get to know

her and to see if I could detect anything she might be up to just so I could be sure.

"Sure, lemme know where," I texted back.

What a day I had ahead of me. Lunch with Cate, dinner with Greg. Great. All I really wanted to do was runaway with Ben and rest in his arms. I just hoped I could stay in control and not give anything away either at lunch –or most importantly, at dinner. I had so many balls in the air, I felt like a juggler at the circus. But instead of balls, it was fire batons. It was becoming more and more complicated and I wasn't sure what any of these people were really up to—from Serena and Colleen to Greg, and even Cate. Hell, I barely even trusted Toni Lyn. Maybe Annie was right. I just had trouble letting go, letting people in, all because I have some major trust issues. I knew I was changing. I also knew I needed to change.

I sent the pictures to Toni Lyn and a copy to Annie just for fun. All of our hosts would be out at the venue signing autographs that day so I thought she'd enjoy seeing the pictures and maybe she'd have some ideas on where she'd like to be positioned. I would bet money she would want to be in the center of the gazebo—all by herself as a feature. It was my plan too, anyway.

I hit send on the email and made sure I had the promos scheduled and the billboards ready to go and approved. I finished everything up and went into that powder room. Just as I had slid on my fresh pink lipstick, I caught myself in the mirror. I wanted change. I wanted to free myself from this uniform of predictability—these pantsuits, these business pumps. I was sick of being me, all tightly wound and bound up in all my own directives. It was way beyond time. I decided that if I wanted it, I had to start right away. No more dreaming. After lunch I would go shopping and buy something new for that dinner with Greg. Catching him off-guard was a great idea. I could do this. And I would. Greg Galloway would have no idea what hit him after I was finished with him. I suddenly felt powerful. Change was good—and I was long overdue. And I suddenly felt like it was now or never.

I knew it wouldn't be as easy to change my attitude as would be to change my outfit. But I was sure willing to try!

CHAPTER TWENTY-SIX

The bright sunshine had warmed the spring day making it almost feel like summer. I wasn't really looking forward to lunch with Cate but I wasn't the type to ever go back on my word. It was a rule. I had asked her to lunch so we would go to lunch. That's just the way it was. Plus, Annie was going and she was such a talker, I knew she could fill in all the dead awkward pieces of conversation. Annie was trained to do that. If there was dead air, she would fill it up. It was her nature— her talent—all part of being a talk show host—no awkward silences.

We all went to this great new restaurant in town, the R. Davidson Chophouse. It had just opened right where the old place, called Tin Top, had been in the center of downtown Tuscaloosa. It had quickly become a favorite of mine. I loved this place and it was a good spot to relax and chat and had such great food—and even better drinks! It had a huge, open dining room with opulent, grand thirty-foot ceilings. It was so stunning! Not only was the atmosphere completely unique, the food was dripping with deliciousness! Cate ordered sangria and I had my usual mimosa but with cranberry juice this time. Annie stuck with her favorite, a salty margarita. If you wanted great drinks, this place was known to have the best mixologist in town! We all sat down in the airy dining room and ordered. The food here was unlike anywhere in town! I ordered the lobster mac and cheese, Cate had the pasta primavera and Annie just loved the Korean BBQ tacos. We ordered a couple of appetizers of crab-cakes, my all-time favorite appetizer, to share. The airy atmosphere with the long sheers over the floor to ceiling windows relaxed me instantly. It was just what I needed. I was actually excited to get into things with Cate. I wanted to get to know her but still felt a tad uneasy for some reason. I wasn't sure how to really find out all I needed to know. So I just jumped right in.

"I am so glad to have you on board for another week," I began. "I think this way I can really see if you're a good fit and you can see if you really like the job."

"Oh, I already know I like the job. I have been waiting for an opportunity like this. I just hope I can be what you need," Cate responded. It was too perfect. I was immediately suspicious. But I was always suspicious.

"Well, you have done very well so far," I answered back reassuringly. "So, Cate, tell me about you—I want to know all about you and your sister," I added.

"I think it's so interesting that we are all twins. That's just fabulous," Annie broke in helping the natural flow of conversation.

"Oh, well Colleen and I aren't that close," Cate explained. "She does her thing and I do mine. I mean, we used to be pretty close, but she kind of wanted to do something different and we had some issues so she went her way and I went mine."

"Oh, well, you do still speak, right?" Annie asked.

"Oh of course. I just kinda think I actually do better on my own. For most of our lives we were inseparable, finishing each other's sentences kinda thing. I think the separation has done me good. I sorta like finishing my own sentences," she laughed as she took a sip of her sangria.

"Annie and I were never like that. We're twins but have always been so different," I said.

"Well, that's not really a bad thing. A person can disappear behind their twin if they aren't the loudest one, you know?"

I was really learning a lot about Cate, and I had to admit it was surprising. I wasn't sure it was real. It could have been a big cover, trying to show she and Colleen weren't possibly conspiring. Here is my trust issue popping up. But here was Annie, smiling and chatting away like Cate was her new bestie. I loved her ease with people. And I loved how she could always make people feel comfortable enough to open up and spill their inner most secrets. I easily distrusted people but Annie instantly created an atmosphere of trust. Surely this is from our childhood. She was always trying to make me comfortable enough to trust things. I shook my head at this thought.

I sat there thinking the worst while Annie was creating that atmosphere of trust and comfort. I listened. Annie had her talents and they made her the star she was. I had other talents. I watched the body language. I watched her eyes as she spoke about her sister, her life and then this—

"It was weird that we both went into the same thing, TV news," Cate divulged.

"Colleen was really good. I guess I was better behind the scenes and now it's my turn to shine. I think the PR world is where I belong. Maybe or maybe not for Colleen. I guess we'll see."

Annie shot me a look. She and I both sensed the obvious competitiveness Cate was feeling with her sister. Maybe even some animosity. It could be an act, but if it was she deserved an Oscar. Again.

"Ever hear anything about how she likes it over there at WRBI?" I asked nonchalantly trying to act like it was a throw away question. It was actually the most important question of the lunch date.

"Not too much," she responded. "I just know she's got some sorta thing for that man she works for. I think they're dating now. That was all she talked about for the longest—that guy—what's his name—she was hot for him and had wanted to work with him forever. Now she's got 'im. Good luck," Cate laughed and nodded her head.

"Greg Galloway," I popped.

"Yeah, that's him. Oh well, she can have 'im. We all knew him in college and he was sort of a jerk sometimes." Cate took a bite of her chicken salad. This was it—all the info I needed to know.

"Oh my Lord," Annie interrupted. "Colleen must be an idiot, bless her heart. I mean everyone knows that Greg guy is a total player."

"I know, but you could never tell Colleen a damn thing. She's a know-it-all so let her hang herself. I tried to rescue her so many times from bad men. The only good man she ever had was Ben Flannigan. And she two-timed him and broke his heart."

I suddenly choked on a pecan. I could barely breathe. I was hacking and causing a scene.

"Are you okay, Abby?" Drink something quick," Annie exploded pushing my water toward me.

I kept choking but finally managed, "I'm fine! Just swallowed wrong. I'll be fine."

What had I just heard? Oh my God, I had all this new information and most importantly, I totally knew I could trust Cate. She would have never said all that if she were spying for her sister. I never knew why Ben and Colleen had broken up. Ben never talked about it and I was scared to bring up something that could be so painful to him. But wow. I was pretty stunned by all Cate had just said. She had no idea I was seeing Ben, and now the thought of seeing Greg for dinner made my stomach twist. I couldn't eat another bite. I felt like I was suffocating under all this secrecy. This wasn't my style at all. My nerves began to take over as I started to clean the table for the waiter.

I wadded up my napkin and wiped the table then grabbed

Cate and Annie's napkins and wiped their spots around their plates. I felt anxious and Annie knew this was what I do when the anxiety sets in—I start cleaning. I am totally OCD when it comes to things being neat anyway. I didn't even realize what I was doing. Annie shot me a look.

Cate didn't seem to notice, she had already had two sangrias. I was on my second mimosa, with added triple sec, and Annie was still mostly just licking the salt off her margarita glass. I needed to end this and get out of there but Annie kept right on filling the dead air. I gave her a look with my eyebrows up. She knew if I was already cleaning the table I was ready to run. The waiter arrived with more water. Water? I wanted more champagne in my mimosa.

"Oh wow, look at you, you already cleaned up for me," he said full of sarcasm. "Wanna a job?"

"Maybe," I grinned. I hadn't even realized what I had done. I would have grabbed their plates from them too if Annie hadn't reached over and pinched my arm.

"Well I need to run," I said. "I have a few places I need to stop on the way back. I hate to rush y'all." We had all ridden over together. That was, in hind site, pretty stupid. I always liked to have my car. That way I could stay in control. But today I had a tipsy Cate and a slow-eating-cause-she's-mostly-talking Annie to drive back to the station before I could have a minute to myself. I needed to sort it all out. Think about my strategy for my dinner with Greg.

The chatter continued for only a tad longer before Cate announced she was full and Annie had licked the last grain of salt from her glass. I paid the bill and drove them back to the station. Two drinks and that wasn't what had even gotten to me—it was that last comment about Ben. Cate got out of my car and made her way to the front door of the radio station. Annie and I sat in the car. We could finally talk with candor.

"Honey, you were a hot mess," Annie said shaking her head. "All that incessant cleaning. What the hell?"

"I know it. But when Cate said Ben had been left because

Colleen cheated on him, I almost lost it," I explained.

"You mean you didn't know?" Annie seemed surprised.

"No, did you?" I asked her.

"No but I would have thought you would have asked him by now," Annie surmised.

"I didn't want to bring up anything more painful than my own break-up with him." I was trying to process it all as I spoke.

"I understand, sweetie. But guzzling that second mimosa was pretty telling. I knew you were losing it" Annie consoled. "And then I thought you were fixin' to head back to wash the dishes yourself with all that tidying up the table. Why would Ben's break-up with Colleen matter so much?"

"It just made me think, you know me. I take it all too seriously I'm sure."

"What did it make you think?" Annie questioned.

"Well, if Ben broke up with Colleen because she was cheating on him, then maybe he really loved her and would still be with her if she hadn't cheated. I suddenly felt like a consolation prize."

"Abby, you are ridiculous! Ben has always loved you. He never stopped. *Colleen* was his consolation prize."

"I love you for saying that but really, he probably wouldn't have left her had he not caught her. They were engaged for heaven's sake!"

I felt nervous. I knew I had to talk to Ben. I couldn't get the thoughts to stop swirling in my head. I didn't want him to think I had any doubts about his feelings for me but I had to know how it had all ended with Colleen. Was I what he really wanted? And then there was me—going out with Greg now behind his back even though it was for work, I kept telling myself. What was I doing? I felt for Ben. He had been treated so badly. First by me, then by Colleen, and now I wasn't being honest with him about Greg. There was nothing I could do now. I had to go get some new clothes and get on with this date. This fake date with Greg, the player. I would just have to explain it all to Ben later. Explain later—that was almost never a good strategy.

CHAPTER TWENTY-SEVEN

The cornflower blue skies had turned to bruised and gray. The clouds were bloated, opening up as I drove into Belk's parking lot, the rain falling and sweeping everything into a flurry of shoppers running to their cars, holding bags overhead. Steam rose above the black pavement from the hot day giving way to the cooling rain. I sat in my car waiting for it to let up before I got out. Clouds continued to gather overhead and the stark shadows of the bright hot sun turned to water-colored paintings in pastel— blurred into the puddles of rainwater collecting on my windshield. I watched as I sat still in my little BMW, the hard rain tapping on my roof. I took peace in the little refuge I had for a moment—breathing slowed and thoughts collected, I knew I had to do what was planned that night with Greg. For some reason Greg wanted to see me. He had asked me at the restaurant before he knew about Ben. Before I knew about Serena. And certainly before I knew about Colleen.

The rain rushed me back to a carefree day in the early summer when I was only seventeen. It was nearing the end of my teenage years. I closed my eyes while I sat in my car and could still smell that summer day. The magnolias blossomed into perfumed white satin, the grass had turned emerald after the fallen rain, fragrant from having been freshly mown just before the skies ripped opened with a clap of thunder. I felt so much like the girl I was back then—the sensual lure of reinvention—to become who I dreamed of being, tugging at me from the inside. I remember sitting on Granny Cartwright's front porch watching the skies swirl and churn and knowing that after this most ordinary yet pivotal day, I would be changed forever, aware that I was growing up and all of us were in a kind of metamorphosis.

The raindrops slowed to a sprinkle and I got out of my car, leaving my memories alone for now, knowing what I had in front of me. I ran inside the department store, filled with swimsuits and colorful beach towels, sparkly flip-flops, everyone getting ready for the annual race to the blue-green gulf. It was a ritual in Alabama. One that I had always cherished. I suddenly couldn't remember the last time I had been to the beach.

I grabbed a prissy skirt in pale baby blue and a white sweater and tank-top ensemble, speckled in tiny hot pink roses. So preppy and so not exactly me. But when I tried it on in the dressing room it felt just delicious to be dressed so full of femininity. I rather liked it.

I paid and left, running through the tiny raindrops back to my car and drove back to the station. Just then I got a text. Greg.

I can meet you at 5:30. How bout Cypress Inn?

Perfect. See you then. I texted back.

Annie was still at work though it was late afternoon. I went straight into her office and closed the door.

"That took a while," she quipped. "Find anything?"

"Yep. I'll go try it on real quick." I ran into the downstairs powder room and changed, fluffing my long dark hair. I had grabbed a pearl necklace on my way out of the store just in case. I slipped it around my neck and clasped it closed. I checked myself just before opening the door. It was amazing, the emotional transformation a new style could create. I actually was starting to feel different. Still filled with anxiety, but I felt more alive. It had been forever since I had even tried on new clothes. My uniform was easy. Same size for five years. Same designer. Same old boring self. This new skirt made me feel a sense of excitement. Ever since that day Annie and I went to the quad I knew I needed to try this reinvention. And I knew it would be for the better.

I stepped out into the hallway and slipped quickly into Annie's office.

"Sugar! *Now* it looks like we might be related," she gushed. "I love this skirt," Annie oozed, pushing back from her desk and walking around to face me.

She reached out and touched the soft blue fabric. "You look fabulous!" Annie leaned over and hugged me. "Just be careful. You know Greg and he can be really persuasive. Not to mention charming."

"Oh, Annie, I am out for one thing. Information. Wish me luck. I need to run."

Annie squeezed my hand. "Call me when you get home. I wanna hear everything."

I smiled at her and went out the back door where I had parked my car. I didn't want to run into Cate and cause any curiosity with these clothes on. I was laser focused. I knew I had a job to do, and this night was at the crux of my entire plan—to get Greg to talk so I could find out what I needed to know to finish on top. After this event I planned my getaway—to take a break and maybe, just maybe, join the summer run to the warm waters of the Alabama Gulf coast.

I got to Cypress Inn early and went straight to the bar. I had a plan. No, although drinking did sound promising, I decided a talk with the bartender would be the way to make this night work. I had known her a long time. Suzy Sanders had been a good friend of mine eons ago. She had been here at Cypress Inn for at least ten years. I knew just what to do and I knew she would totally comply.

"Hey girl," I said taking a seat.

"Well looky here at you. Am I really seeing Abby Harper? Queen of the suit? Girl you look amazing? New man?"

"Not exactly. I need your help."

"My help? Oh dear this has got to be good. Okay I'm game, Hon. Spill."

"I'm trying to one up this guy who has stolen ideas from me forever. I know he's gonna be drinking. He'll suspect if I don't drink too and I've already got two mimosas in me from lunch. So I will be ordering drinks but I need mine clean—no alcohol."

"So he's gonna drink himself into spilling his secrets and you will stay sober and in control."

"You got it," I affirmed.

"Girl, I like the way you think," Suzy smiled. "Deal. He can keep drinking and all those mimosas will be just O.J. Great plan."

I glanced down at my watch. He should be here any moment. I wanted a table near the bar so I went to the hostess desk and asked to be seated first so I could pick the spot before Greg arrived. I took my seat near the window where I could see the bar and watch the meandering Warrior River. The inky water lapped against the banks as the Bama Belle Riverboat made its way home for night.

My mind began to wander thinking about Greg and our uncanny history. On and off and never really any true love. Those early days in college I was still just a girl. He was so confident and in charge. I liked that. It made him seem so masculine at the time. I had to wonder why he was so insistent on seeing me. If it were true that he was seeing both Colleen and Serena, why in the world did he want me in the mix? It was baffling. Was he really interested in me, just another notch in his belt so to speak? Or was he trying to make one of them jealous? One thing was certain, I was sure to find out. He was here.

I saw him come through the front door and the hostess showed him to our table.

"Look at you," he began. "You look great! Where's the suit?" He teased, seating himself. His large frame and broad shoulders already turning heads. And those dimples. Deep and perfect framing his cute smile. What a cover he had. For I knew underneath all that masculine perception laid a snake in waiting. I had to keep my guard up and stay focused.

"Oh, I don't always wear suits anymore," I retorted. "Not always in style anymore." I smiled as the waiter approached and took our drink orders. Greg ordered his usual; Makers Mark and I ordered my mimosa. O.J.

"Well I might say the change sure looks good on you," he grinned.

"Thanks. But I thought you were seeing that Serena girl. At least that's what she said."

"How do you know her anyway?" I was saved from answering when the waiter arrived back with our water. "Be right back with the bar order," he said.

"Uhm, well she actually had misdialed me and I texted her thinking I was texting someone else since her number was in my phone." I thought for a second and I was actually proud of that quick comeback.

"Oh yeah she didn't seem to know either," he said as he took a sip of water.

I was sure she didn't, especially since right before Greg had shown up I had let her know just who she was dealing with confronting her on canceling the venue. Undercover of course. But I knew she wouldn't want Greg to know she had screwed up if he was actually involved in her dirty work.

The waiter showed up with the drinks and upon first sip I knew I had only orange juice in that—ahem, mimosa. I looked over my shoulder at Suzy in the bar and she winked at me. Greg guzzled his down as we awkwardly looked over the menus. I had been here a hundred times. I could recite the menu in my sleep. Cypress Inn was a Tuscaloosa staple, the only really nice upscale spot on the river for the longest time with its own gazebo and huge windows placed perfectly so you almost always had a fabulous view of the mighty river from your seat. I loved this place. The seafood was delicious and the sides and starters were all southern and tasty.

The waiter returned and took our orders, scallops for me with a starter of fried green tomatoes. Greg ordered the catfish and another Makers Mark.

"So," I began, "tell me all about your new girl, Serena. She seemed nice."

"Oh she is but she's reading way too much into this. I just met her and already she's hearing wedding bells. Tell ya the truth, I've only gone out with her once."

"Well she surely does like you. And she's excited about what she thinks are mutual feelings," I said grinning back at him. I so wanted to make him squirm. A few more drinks in him and I could talk about Colleen.

Greg gazed over at me, his eyes glistening as he leaned in over the table as if to whisper. "I don't really wanna talk about Serena, Abby. What I really wanna talk about is you."

Oh God, I sighed to myself. *Here we go.* The schmoozing and charming was oozing out but this time it was all hitting a wall.

But, I knew I had to play the game. So I leaned in close to him. "Okay, I'm in," I said my eyebrows up letting him know I was ready to hear everything he had to say.

Greg swigged his whisky and smiled at me like he could eat me up in one bite. "Whatdya wanna know?" I asked playfully.

"So, are you seeing Benny these days?" He asked condescendingly. He never liked Ben. It was kind of a good versus evil thing. The minute I wound up going out with Ben, eventually moving in with him during senior year, it had been a battle between the two of them. And the fact that I had only been intimate with the two of them had made things sorta sticky for me. Greg had been my first lover but I almost married Ben. But how to answer this question so Greg wouldn't close up? I needed him to feel free to talk.

"No not really. We ran into each other a few weeks ago. Its pretty causal."

"So you're not seeing anyone right now?"

"Nope, just too busy."

"Huh, well I would have never guessed you'd be unattached at the moment," Greg said swigging the last drop of the amber liquid and signaling for another.

"Don't you need another?" He asked as he studied my nearly empty glass. Greg was never one to drink alone.

"Sure, why not?" I agreed.

The waiter nodded and headed back to the bar. I glanced over and Suzy gave me another wink. Still safe. I let out a breath but made sure Greg couldn't see me relax. I wanted him to think I was nervous so he'd feel like he was on top. Greg always had to be on top. For every single possible event. Ahem. That was where we clashed. Who was in control? We both wanted, no, needed to be.

The drinks arrived and so did the appetizers. Greg was on his third drink and I was on my second glass on O.J. I decided to swig it down so he would think I was drinking more and I started to giggle here and there so he would think the alcohol was getting to me. He knew I could never hold more than two glasses.

"So maybe we could go back to my place and have a little nightcap?" he gleamed. And with that the food arrived. Thank God. I had no idea how to answer but I knew for certain I was headed for trouble.

CHAPTER TWENTY-EIGHT

Midway through my scallops my glass was empty and Greg ordered another round for both of us, without even asking me. Just to be on the safe side, I looked over at the bar to reassure myself. No Suzy! Ohmygod! And here comes my drink.

May I just say as a rule, Orange Juice does not mix well with fried seafood.

The waiter put down the drinks and left as I immediately picked mine up and smelled it. Yep full of champagne and a healthy dose of triple sec. I sipped my water now full of melted ice.

"You didn't ever answer my question. Nightcap?"

"Oh Greg, seriously you know I've had enough. I won't even be able to drive. And you certainly shouldn't. Maybe another time."

I could sense he was a tad tipsy. I took my chances. "I heard that Colleen Cantrell was working for you these days."

"She is. And so strange I heard that her twin sister was working for you. Small world."

"Indeed." Shit. He was still on top of the game. I tried again. "A little birdy also told me you were seeing her. So, are you?"

"Oh, I see," he mused. "You need to know if I'm free before you agree to see me too. You are such a little sneak."

He didn't know the half of it.

"I sure am, silly boy. You know I was never interested in being someone's affair. So, tell me all about Colleen," I pushed, hoping he would let something slip.

"Well I was seeing her pretty regularly. But she got mad 'cause she saw me flirtin' with someone. Well, she thought I was flirtin'."

"Were you? I'm gonna throw out a wild guess here but I think yes. Right?"

"Well you know, I wasn't meaning to. Things just happen. Look I really am sorry about everything we've been through. Come on. Let's have a little dessert somewhere. You're probably right—we don't need to drink anymore. Well I know you don't."

I giggled playing right along. I wanted to know more about the event and at this point I was willing to do whatever I needed to get in order get the info. He was just starting to talk. "Well okay," I offered, "but why don't we just go out to the gazebo or the dock here and have it. That way we don't have to drive," I offered.

"Perfect. Let's order something and take it outside to the dock," he surmised. "It's a beautiful night after all that sudden rain today. Cooled off a bit. Abby, I really hope you know I'm not playing games with you. I really do hope we can see where this leads."

It's gonna lead to nowhere but not until you tell me just what you know.

"Sounds like a plan," I played along. We ordered desserts, smothered in gooey chocolate and Greg paid the bill. We took our small plates and headed outside, following the lighted path toward the dark river. The dock was lit in little amber lights creating the perfect atmosphere for Greg to spill his secrets. The cool of the evening surrounded us, humid air wrapping us in a damp blanket. The river lapped the banks building an intoxicating rhythm under the dock.

I knew I had him. He was giggly and loose and though I acted like I was too, I was in complete control and ready to hear everything he had to say. What I wasn't ready for was just how aggressive he would be.

We sat down on the wooden benches. Greg immediately moved closer to me. The smell of alcohol lingered on his breath. My heartbeat quickened as I felt his muscular thigh against mine, pushing in to sit closer and closer to me.

"So tell me," he began, "you still miss me?"

"I do sometimes," I leaned closer to him.

"Well we need a cure for that, I'd say," he teased.

Greg set his plate down and turned toward me with a hungry look in his eyes. It scared me a little because now I felt like I belonged to Ben. I hadn't felt this before. I swallowed hard. I knew what he had planned for the rest of the evening. I also knew I had to play along if I wanted him to spill anything that might help me. Still, instinctively I pulled back as he leaned forward.

"Aww, c'mon now, don't tease me. You know you've missed me somethin' awful," he pushed. Greg was still drinking, the glass sitting next to him on the bench.

"You have to play the game," I kept telling myself. I grinned at him, and leaned in close enough to feel his breath on my lips. I was expecting a sudden hard attack-like kiss, but Greg was sometimes unpredictable. He leaned in slowly and kissed me gently, his warm lips in stark contrast to the cool damp night air. I let him linger, tasting me seductively.

He pulled back and smiled at me. "Now that's more like it," he oozed.

I knew it was safe to go in for the kill.

I leaned in and kissed him slightly, my tongue licking his bottom lip. I looked up and gazed into his eyes, "So what would Colleen and Serena think about this?" I asked as I kept kissing him.

"Who cares about them right now? Let's just put it this

way, they serve their purpose."

Okay, he was using them both to get what he wanted.

"And just what purpose is that?" I asked nuzzling his face, kissing him softly on his cheeks, then his lips.

"You know, just certain things I need. I know you're not dumb Abby."

"No, tell me. You mean physical needs?" I kissed him on his hungry mouth to disguise the question.

"That and more," he answered. But it wasn't enough. I needed more. I was waiting to hear how he used Serena to try to cancel my venue; I was waiting to hear how he had used Colleen to try to push her sister to spy on me. How he always managed to steal my plans and one-up me on every single promotion we had done over the last few year. How he would steel my football stars and other city celebrities to be the draw for his events. I hated that I couldn't get anything concrete out of him. I wasn't giving up. I had to get what I needed. I would use him in his most vulnerable places if I had to.

"C'mon, now who's being the tease? You can tell me, baby. I know those girls don't mean a thing to you. What all have they been doing to make you –uhm, happy?" I slid my fingers up his thigh, and rested my hand very near his now throbbing cock. Just close enough to drive him crazy.

"Oh Abby, you know me all too well. Those girls do exactly what I need, whenever I need it. Not just the physical, but the whole world of my needs, and you know I have needs baby."

I felt his tongue on my lips; reluctantly I opened my mouth and let him in. He kissed me deeply and passionately and I almost felt as if I was losing myself in this act. Greg was purely intoxicating. I had to pull back before it was too late.

"You sure do have needs," I whispered. "But just how do they fulfill them all, just the two of them?"

"You know, Abby. You know." Suddenly he pulled away, slipping his large hands around my waist he pulled me across his lap. I was straddling his large bulge and as hard as I was trying it was nearly impossible not to lose myself in this heat. He was commanding and forceful. I had to be careful.

"No, I don't know why don't you tell me all about what they do for you. How can I compete if I don't know what I'm up against?" I asked as I kissed him over and over. I could sense he was slipping. He was going to let me into his secrets, spill himself in more ways than one. I felt the shift. I was winning.

"I'll tell you everything you want to know if you do me one favor," he promised in a sexy whisper.

"Anything," I said as I licked his lips.

"Why don't you tell me all about Cate. And just how you really wound up with Serena the other night. Huh? If we share secrets and work together we could be quite the power couple."

"What?"

"Baby, think about it. You tell me and I'll tell you."

I quickly swung my leg backwards and dismounted. My mind was racing a million miles an hour. What had I just heard? Was he playing *me*? All this time I thought I had him and all this time he had been playing me? *Oh Abby, you are such an idiot,* I thought. How could I be so stupid? So I was there to get something—the same thing Greg was there to get. It all became suddenly clear.

"Hey baby, what's this? You don't wanna tell old Greg what all is going on? Come on."

"Now I see why you asked me out. Why you were so insistent on seeing me tonight. You didn't really want to see me, you wanted to get me drunk and hoped I'd spill my secrets."

"And hmm, just who does that remind you of? We're two of a kind Abby. Surely you see that?" He chortled.

I stood up, feeling an anger inside me rise and nearly choke me. I was so mad I could have spit nails. But I refused to let him see it. I suddenly had an idea.

"Oh, Greg, you have always been right. C'mere baby. I still want to fill those needs you have."

"I knew you'd see things my way," he said sounding like the big bad wolf.

Greg stood up and grabbed me tightly against his big hard body, kissing me passionately like he could devour me. I kissed him back moving my body around to switch places with him so he would be up against the rail of the dock. I kept kissing him backing him up until, whoops…Greg got the ultimate cold shoulder. He hit the Warrior River with a mighty splash.

"Uh oh. I guess you needed to cool off. That should help."

I turned and left him in the frigid water. And yes, it felt great!

CHAPTER TWENTY-NINE

I pulled into my driveway, exhausted and disgusted with myself. How did I not see through the entire act? Greg was doing exactly what I was doing, and that in itself totally made me nauseated. Was he right? Were we really just alike? I made my way to the front door, immediately noticing the azaleas missing and the porch nicely swept clean. I walked to the right of my porch and looked down the side of the house, all the blossoms planted neatly in a row, the ground freshly wet from the rains that afternoon. I smiled to myself as I made my way to the door, and unlocked it, stepping inside, safe from the nightmare I had just lived. I was mad and so frustrated.

Gertie greeted me with a purr and an arched back. I locked my door as if to block the world away. I felt defeated. Outsmarted. Like, as always, Greg finished on top. And I let myself get even the slightest bit turned on by him. I almost threw up I was so sick and mad at myself. I put some coffee on and went upstairs to change out of my new look and into my most comfy pajamas. They were stained and faded but I felt safe and warm. I just wanted to be in that place of quiet solitude where I could just be me and not have to put on any show. I had to think and process and be still for a minute.

But it wouldn't last. As I made my way back downstairs to

join my fresh cup of coffee for a date on the dimly lit kitchen, I suddenly heard the phone ring. I arrived in the kitchen just in time to catch the caller ID. Dixie. I let the machine get it.

"Hey Zelda, this is Flannery—you know, Dixie Darlene, (She giggles) I just wanted to remind you about Book Club. We moved it again back to Friday and you, girlfriend, have doughnut duty. I just can't wait to see you girl! It's at 7 o'clock at my house. See you then honey, bye."

"Oh Flannery, I swear, I don't freakin' care. Bye yourself." I said into the quiet of the house to myself. I felt like such an idiot. All I knew was I just really wanted out of all of this. Greg got the better of me tonight. I remembered I was supposed to call Annie and fill her in. I didn't feel much like talking, especially reliving the evening, and having to admit defeat. I sent her a text.

"It didn't go quite as planned. See you tomorrow."

"I'm coming over," she texted back. *"Matt had to go into the store. One of his managers quit. I'm bringing food so don't go to bed."* Matt owned an outdoor and camping shop downtown. And I knew Annie. Once she decided to do something there was no talking her out of it. I shuffled to the kitchen and made extra coffee. I kept the lights as dim as possible. I didn't much feel like doing anything but hiding. That was until Annie arrived. She was actually in pajamas too. Of course hers were pink and cute with little clouds all over them. I had to admit I was so relieved to see her, and of course the sweet confections she brought along with her.

"Hey sweetie, I got *hot now* doughnuts from Krispy Kreme and we're gonna have us a little party, just you and me." She swished past me in her cute little bedroom ensemble and into my little kitchen, setting the warm green polka dot box down on the round wooden table in the center of the room.

"Okay, I admit, you're a sight for sore eyes," I smiled, getting two mugs from the cabinet for our coffee.

"Sit down here and tell me everything," she started. "I need to know exactly what all happened."

I filled Annie in on every tiny detail as we bathed ourselves in the fried sugary concoctions, savoring every flaky bite of sweetness.

"Honey, why in the world would you possibly feel defeated? I mean c'mon sweetie, you, most definitely, left on top—you pushed him into the river and left him there!" Annie laughed as she reached across the table and raised her hand slapping me a huge high-five midair.

"Girl, seriously, you won that round," she assured.

Annie was the best when anyone needed to feel up. She could cheer you, motivate you and make you feel like you could run the world. She was precisely who I needed—and she knew that. Not me. I licked my sticky lips and laughed. "I guess you're right, for all I know his tricky ass is still in that river right this minute."

"See, of course, and you certainly aren't like him, Abby. You have never done a thing like this in your entire life. You were trying to beat him at his own game. You weren't used to it but he was—he totally knew what he was doing. It's second nature to him to be sneaky, almost like breathing. It's in his DNA. Not in yours whatsoever."

"It was just exhausting. I don't have that much energy to be so conniving," I admitted. "He was playing me as I was thinking I was playing him. But he wound up in the river," I smiled again at my sister. "Annie, what would I ever do without you?"

"Well, my dear, you will never have to know." She raised her coffee cup as I followed her lead and raised mine. They clinked together in a toast to us. Annie had always been my best friend. She was much more outgoing and her BFF had been CarolAnn for as long as I could remember. I never had a real female best friend. I was much less social and more to myself than Annie. And really, who could I be more myself around than Annie, and who would have my back better than her? She was my twin, and my BFF. And again, she proved herself that night, sitting in my kitchen in our pajamas licking friend dough from our sugary lips and laughing late into the night. It was a harrowing night that had turned into a warm memory, all because of Annie.

We were still giggling and shoveling a final doughnut into our mouths when my cell rang in my purse. I reached over to the countertop and pulled it out of the inside pocket of my bag. It was Ben.

"Hi Sweetheart, everything okay?"

"No, my horse is sick and the race is coming up fast. My sister is caring for her but it looks bad. I need to get up there. I'm gonna leave Saturday evening. Can you come with me?"

"Oh no, Ben that's awful. Of course I'll come. What time?"

"I have a morning breakfast meeting I can't miss so how 'bout three o'clock? I'll come get you."

"Okay, baby. I know she's gonna be okay. Your sister is really good and she's in good care with her. I'll be ready by 3."

"Thanks Abby, I love you."

"Love you too."

He hung up and I filled Annie in about what all was happening with Ben's derby horse.

"Oh no, I'm so sorry, she said. It's gonna be okay. I know it. Really don't worry. Get through the day tomorrow. And get ready to go on Saturday. He'll need you and you can use this time to visit with his family. You haven't seen them since…"

"Don't say it. It was the most horrible day of my life. It will be super hard to see them again. I know there's no love lost there. I wonder if Ben's even told his mom he's seeing me again."

"I think you better ask him so you can prepare yourself. It wouldn't be fair if you didn't know."

"You're right. You are pretty insightful you know?"

"Goes along with the job, both on the air—and with being your sister," she smirked.

It had gotten late. I was beyond exhausted. And I knew Annie was tired but with her bubbly energy, you'd never know it. "Go home and get some sleep. Oh, did you ever go through all those pictures from The Battle Friedman Home?"

"No, but I'm planning to before the show tomorrow. I'll choose a few to make the newspaper ads to promote my show. I'll see you in the morning. Get some sleep sweetheart." Annie got up and I slid my chair back to walk her to the front door.

"Thanks for coming to my rescue," I smiled and gave her a hug.

"Of course, you've done the same for me a hundred times. That's what we do." She kissed my cheek and hugged me back.

I watched Annie walk to her car and get in, the car motor interrupting the quiet late night. Just as I was closing the door I glanced to the left and saw Mitzy making her way up her steps dragging her suitcase behind her. She stopped and looked down. Then I heard a scream. Oh Lord, she was out of town and never saw my cryptic directive, the one I now regretted, spray-painted in hot pink on her porch. I quickly turned off the lights and ran upstairs. Gertie snuggled into bed next to me. The house was pitch black and quiet, when suddenly I heard the tale tell signs of certain trouble—police sirens pulling up in front of Mitzi's house. Could this day ever end?

CHAPTER THIRTY

I tied hard to fall asleep. I lay still and listened carefully trying to decipher anything I could. Mitzy was screaming and putting on quite the show. I could hear her fake crying all the way up to my bedroom windows. I almost wet my bed when I heard her say she knew who did it.

"But Officer, I am quite sure this person did it."

But then I heard the officer reply, "Well, Ms. Montgomery, if you were out of town overnight, how could you have seen who did this? You did say you had just gotten home and saw this—er, uhm, *greeting*. You also said it wasn't there when you left. So there's no way for you to know who the person with this spectacular vocabulary is, right?"

"I guess I have no proof," Mitzy acquiesced.

"We'll do a little investigating tomorrow. My partner has taken plenty of pictures. We'll be back in touch next week," the officer promised.

The policemen left. I heard their tires crunch the gravel of the long drive. Mitzy was livid. I snuck out of bed and crept over to the window peeking out. I could see her front porch and the hot pink message. Mitzy glared up at my windows. I prayed she didn't catch me standing there looking at her.

"I'll have the last word you royal bitch. You'll see." She

said it loud enough for me to hear. God, I dreaded getting up the next morning—what in the world would I wake up to next?

* * *

Hazy sunlight streamed through the puddled pale blue curtains of my windows. I dressed quickly and ran downstairs. I was running late. I fed Gertrude and opened the front door, to this little note from Mitzy. No envelope. No Salutations. Just a ripped piece of notebook paper with this nice little message.

You think you're so smart, do you? Well the life coach in me knows better than to lower myself to play in your little filthy playground Ms. Harper, but to quote your graffiti, BITE ME too. Just know I am watching you inside your house and through my peephole. I will never stop watching you Ms. Harper. I will spend today sifting through your things looking for evidence of hot pink paint—and don't you worry, I'll be bringing Al Roker with me. He is not to be denied and your Gertrude will pay for not allowing him to do what is natural for a specimen like my Al Roker. You'd better hide and take that overweight bitchy tease of a cat with you.
Like the song says, Ms. Harper, I'll be watching you.
Mitzy.

I immediately went to garage and grabbed the can of spray paint, and stuffed it inside my bag. I made sure all my doors were locked and before I could help myself I scribbled a note to Mitzy.

Dear Ms. Montgomery,
I have consulted my own life coach. I felt you to be unqualified since you cannot control yourself. She has convinced me that it is easier to ask forgiveness than to seek permission. So do forgive me for the note I have left you today.

*By the way, I hope your Al Roker goes savage on you and
claws your beady little eyes out!*
   Here's a new directive for you: SUCK IT.
   Good day.

I put the note into my bag and left my house, locking the
door behind me. I backed out of my driveway, and rolled to a
stop in front of Mitzy's mailbox. I reached over and opened her
box and put the note inside and sped away, gravel spewing
behind me. Mitzy was the last thing I needed and the very
worst way to start this day.

I had woken up late that day because I tossed and turned
all night and it wasn't because of my nasty neighbor and the
police. It was because of the overwhelming guilt I felt from
making out with Greg the night before. It was going to eat me
alive if I didn't come clean. I hated that I even did it all but
what I hated most was that I was even mildly starting to enjoy
it. I felt like Greg still had a hold over me. He could still get to
me. I felt weak and that wasn't something I was used to
feeling. And that in itself made me feel even worse.

I made it to work barely thinking about the drive. I was on
autopilot. I barely saw anyone staying holed up in my office
and then I decided to go home early. Annie popped in just
before I left.

"You look like hell, sugar. You sick?"

"No, it's just that psychopathic neighbor of mine. No
biggie."

"Abby, you seriously think you can lie to me? C'mon."

"Shut the door," I pressed. "Okay," I began, "I guess I just
can't shake this guilt. I wanted to get some info outta Greg but
I was enjoying all that heated handsy passion Greg has always
delivered. I wish I hadn't but I did."

"Look at me," Annie demanded in her most stern voice.
"You're human. Anyone in the throws of passion with
someone you find so deliriously attractive would get excited in
the moment. It doesn't mean you have feelings for him. It

simply means you're alive."

"But I love Ben. I do."

"Of course you do. I see that look in your eyes when you talk about him. C'mon, Abby, passion isn't love. Making out with an attractive man I can easily see how you could get carried away when you were in the position you were in last night. Let it go. It didn't mean anything."

"I'm trying. It's just hard. I never want to hurt Ben again."

"Listen to me. You will. And he will hurt you. Hurting is part of living. You will both be hurt and you will both forgive and you will go on. We are living beings and hurting and sadness and joy and love are all part of the messy mix of being alive. Go home. And Abby, try to get out of your own way, at least a little."

"You sound like a psychologist, or a life coach."

"I play one on the radio, remember?"

Annie smiled and made her way to my office door. "I'm fixin' to go through that last round of pictures and I'll be sending them tonight," she added.

"Okay, I'll be at Book Club. I have doughnut duty."

Annie burst out laughing. "I know, and you are who this month? Zelda? Okay just remember, Zelda was the crazy one."

"Only because a man made her that way," I quipped.

"Touché sweetheart."

Annie left as I stood to gather my things. Home, at least for a few hours was what I needed. Safe and alone in the quiet. I needed to think and get it all into perspective. So many changes. I still wanted that. I just couldn't seem to figure out how to make it happen.

* * *

After a couple of hours at home, I was feeling much better. I was actually excited to go to Book Club. It was the roaring twenties so I donned a sliver sequined ankle length shift I had worn to a roaring twenties party last year and wrapped a black headband around my forehead and clipped a pale blue feather just above my ear.

Blue is certainly my color. I had always chosen it while Annie consistently chose pink. It was simple; blue was the color of the sky, my favorite place to drift off. Especially the twilight skies of dusk when the stars first begin to twinkle and show off their brilliance. A spritz of Flowerbomb perfume on my wrists and neck and I was off to Book Club. I went to the drive-through at Krispy Kreme on the corner of 15th Street and McFarland Boulevard. The Hot Now sign was lit in crimson as I pulled in to get the standard three dozen for the afternoon. There were seven of us, plus one new member but Dixie said she was on a diet. Only get one for her. I knew she'd eat three.

Annie had cheered me up and time alone at home had recharged my batteries. Even Mitzy had stayed on her side of the alley. I was poised and ready for a good day with the ladies. I pulled into the long drive of Dixie's home, a gorgeous southern-styled mansion complete with white columns and a wide front porch. Her husband was the Dean of Engineering at the University and she was a beauty consultant for Mary Kay. She was also president of the junior league, the Ladies Auxiliary and the Women of Indian Hills Country Club. All of this is code for Busy Body. I walked up the long sidewalk, my pale blue purse hanging from my wrist holding the boxes of hot sugary goodness.

I managed the doorbell. Dixie flung it open with a huge grin.

"Hey there Zelda, get on in here," she popped. "Only a few ladies are here so far. I'm so glad you could make it." Dixie was perky like always. I stepped inside the well appointed home and found Eleanor, Judith and Rita sitting on the yellow striped sofa under the back window facing the golf course. They were going by the names of Coco Channel, Amelia Earhart and Clara Bow, respectively. Normally they liked to go by the names of the original Destiny's Child. They were all old and filthy rich. All old money left to them by their rich families. Land money dating back to before the Civil War. The oldest of the bunch was Eleanor. She usually dozed off by the middle of the readings. I think we bored her to sleep. I met her a few years back at an event for mystery authors. Can you believe that frail tiny little lady who had skin like crepe paper loved Stephen King? You know, Cujo? That insane attack dog? He wrote mostly horror not even mystery. Her love of blood and death was the real mystery. Judith and Rita were sweeter but mostly ran around after Eleanor refilling her Jack Daniels with a splash of water.

Clara arrived in full out twenties regalia. She dressed like this though for every meeting. Her Book Club name was Gertrude Stein. She, at least, thought she was the most important person in the room. Janie was sitting next to her. She was young and beautiful with long shiny brown hair. She was calling herself Ella Fitzgerald. Because she thought she could sing. *Thought.* She continuously volunteered to sing the national anthem each week. This was no different.

"Sit down, Janie. This isn't a baseball game. We don't need The Star Spangled Banner every week," Dixie snapped.

"Oh please, then let me sing Stars Fell On Alabama," Clare shouted wiping the doughnut off her mouth with the sleeve of her flapper dress.

"Okay, not a bad idea since we are celebrating the roaring twenties," Dixie surmised. "Let's all stand."

Stars Fell On Alabama was the state song. We were all standing and singing as Dixie took to the grand piano to play us through. We were still singing as the new girl walked into the large living room. I suddenly choked. Colleen Cantrell stood ten feet from me. Her glare was so penetrating I felt like a laser was piercing my chest.

CHAPTER THIRTY-ONE

No sooner had we finished up the readings than Colleen made a beeline straight to me. It actually took me aback to be approached with such intensity.

"Look, you're not fooling anyone," she hissed. "I know you were with Greg last night. Even though he was wet with river water he still smelled of that cheap disgusting perfume you're wearing right this minute. When he came home soaking wet I confronted him and he admitted you were trying to seduce him all night. He said he fought you off until you kissed him so hard he fell over the dock and into the river. Then you left him! Who the hell do you think you are? He's not yours anymore."

"He *lives* with you?" I asked astonished.

"Yes he most certainly does. He said he told you that but you just kept coming on to him."

"Honey you certainly have this all wrong. He came on to me. Surely you know him and his reputation," I retorted.

"He has rejected you. The only thing I can do now is to make sure Ben knows who he's really dating these days. You never could make up your mind between them. I know you're seeing Ben now. And he is too nice to suspect you. I've already left him a message to call me." She smirked and with that threat she turned and started to walk away.

Just then Eleanor appeared right behind her. After the dramatic pivot Colleen had made, the two of them were face to face when Eleanor interrupted Colleen's dramatic exit.

"Look here little girl, you make one move to upset my Ben and I will have your ass on a platter. Do you hear me?" Eleanor was a bad-ass.

"Who the hell are you?" Colleen spewed.

"I'm Eleanor Fitzgerald. Ben is my godson. I never did like you. I knew you were always after the Flannigan money. I dropped to my knees and thanked baby Jesus the day Ben let you go. He finally realized what a two-timing slut you really are. Say a word to him about this lady and I will make sure your filthy reputation is splattered all over Tuscaloosa. Are we clear?"

Colleen stood there with her mouth dropped open. I was now smirking at her. She turned with a fast pivot and headed straight for the front door.

I looked at Eleanor. "How do you know all these things?" I asked her.

"It pays to be a nosey old bitch," she grinned.

Sick 'em Cujo.

CHAPTER THIRTY-TWO

I was so anxious I barely slept. I woke with the sunrise and hurried around my room packing for my trip up to North Alabama that afternoon with Ben. I couldn't help thinking of all that had happened at Book Club. I was so shocked but felt so empowered by Eleanor. That was the strength I always had admired in the women I was surrounded by growing up. Even my mom, I have come to understand, always stood up for all of us—even Granny Cartwright and *even* when they weren't getting along.

My older sister Rhonda had that fabulous set of friends all her life, Blake and Vivi. Now they were big time Steel Magnolias. They liked to call themselves Sassy Belles when they were younger and in high school. They were wonderful role models. I always saw how they consistently had each other's backs. I was actually on my way to Vivi's for a meeting that Saturday morning. Blake and Vivi were holding a little planning session for a big shindig on Memorial Day for a local women's shelter. Vivi always had the backs of other women. It was a lunch so I knew I had to be totally ready for Ben by 3pm. I dressed in some casual clothes, red pencil pants and a navy top with ¾ length sleeves. I tied a navy and white polka dot scarf around my head like a headband tied at the shoulder. Red lipstick and white Keds finished the Jackie Kennedy look I had wanted to achieve. It would be perfect to get reacquainted with Ben's family.

I set out food and fresh water for Gertrude and locked the front door, leaving my bags ready in the foyer. Riding out to Vivi's was the most peaceful drive. I rolled my windows down to let the warm fragrant air inside; the springtime was healing and full of hope and promise. Emerald hills crawling with kudzu and pine stretched out for miles in front of me. Green was everywhere this time of year, tumbling down the hillsides to kiss the endless ribbons of blacktop for as far as I could see. The South is so rich in all the most sensual ways. To be here is to have every sense awakened. The perfumed air filled with the fragrance of pine year 'round, the symphonic music of nature in its purest forms, especially on a summer's night. Frogs and crickets delivering a cadence so loud it could echo through the forests of moss and damp grasses, the alto hum of beehives overhead, a brush of damp air on my warm skin on a sultry hot night, the sweet liquid dripping down my throat after taking a bite of the first crisp watermelon picked right from my backyard garden, and all the green that surrounded me most of year. When I visited out west one summer to see the Grand Canyon, I felt my eyes literally hunger for all that green of home.

I knew I wanted to do something else with my life other than compete with Greg over media promos, but I also knew I could never leave the South. I fit here.

I pulled into the long driveway of Vivi's historic old southern plantation. It had been in her family for generations. All the girls were already there. Rhonda, Blake and Vivi were waiting when I got out and made my way up the old steps to the wide and inviting front porch, littered with white wicker, yellow striped cushions and slow whirling fans overhead. Rich green ferns waved gently in the breezes. I wanted to move in.

"Hey ladybug, get over here and give me a hug, Vivi greeted me as I reached the top stair. She was wiping her hands on her apron, her wiry curls caught in the midday breeze. She was a sight for sore eyes. Tiny in stature but the strongest one of the bunch, Vivi was the girl you wanted on your side in a crisis. She was a fierce mother and a fierce friend to those she loved. I was so glad I was in that mix. You sure never wanted Vivi on your bad side. I would place bets she could tear you apart with her bare hands if you hurt someone she loved. She was one of a kind. I had known her almost all of my life and she never changed. Loud and genuine, she would call it like she saw it.

"Hey you, I am so glad you invited me," I said hugging her back.

"Come on in here. We're already drinkin' and it's barely even noon," she laughed.

I turned right and walked through the lavish dining hall and back into the kitchen where everyone was already seated around the oversized wooden table. I felt like I had come home after a long absence. I took a seat next to Blake and across from my sister after hugging everyone hello.

"Girl you aren't even gonna believe this," Vivi exclaimed as she slipped in behind us to the cabinets. She grabbed a wine glass and poured me a shot of Sangria as she talked.

"You know that Martha May Collins from last year's charity drive? Honey she up and died last night. It's the very saddest thing. I had counted on her to make the cupcakes again this year. She waddin' but barely 80."

"Eighty! Honey, that's all but both feet in the grave," Blake interjected. "How long you think people live?"

"Well her mama lived to be a hundred and three. Hell she just died last year." "Well you know what they say?" Vivi popped right back.

"No, what?" Blake asked.

"Folks don't live too long after their closest loved one dies."

"That what people say about married couples," Rhonda interrupted.

"Well Martha May did live with her mother, so I think that rule applies to her too. She died of a broken heart." Rhonda explained.

"No she died of a broken hip," Vivi shot. "She fell a month ago and it was all downhill from there. Either way, poor Martha May."

"Yeah, bless her heart," Blake added.

I smiled to myself listening to the group. I loved this little posse of ladies in the best ways, everything about them made me hungry for more of this—tight-knit friendships, laughter and story-telling. I made a promise to myself I would make an effort to take part in more things with this strong group of Sassy Belles. Annie should do it too. She would fit right in.

"Well, Abby, tell us what all is going on with you these days. I been hearin' good things," Vivi said sitting down next to Rhonda and across from Blake.

"Oh, God, okay Rhonda what have you spilled?" I jumped.

"Sweetie, it's okay. Everybody here is on your side."

I knew that was true. And it sure felt good. In fact I felt so at home and immensely happy I wanted to move into Vivi's and just live in all the love I felt there that day. I was never one to trust people very easily. But in the bosom of this little clan I felt safe. It may be the only place I did besides with Annie.

"Okay, y'all, I'm back with Ben," I blurted and smiled feeling a little embarrassed to be talking out loud about my love life. I had actually never done this before in a crowd of more than... uhm. One.

"Oh honey, that is wonderful. I am so happy for you!" Blake beamed.

"I say let's raise a glass to that," Vivi giggled. All the girls raised their glasses and with a clink they all wished me the best. Suddenly I felt that tinge of guilt over Greg from the other night.

"Oh, honey, why the sudden long face?" Rhonda noticed.

"Oh it's nothing," I answered brushing it off rather quickly. But it didn't take. I really didn't want to get into it but

I knew I was fixin' to.

"C'mon, sugar, you're among friends. Is everything going okay with him?" Blake, ever the lawyer, pushed.

"Oh yes, absolutely. Of course. Ben is even more wonderful than he was all those years ago. I love him. And he told me he loves me too."

"Well honey, of course he does. He never stopped. But you still didn't say why the long face. I know you. What's going on?" I could see Rhonda wasn't gonna let up.

"I did something I'm ashamed of," I divulged. "I'm guilty. I have a confession to make."

"Well I'm certainly no priest but lemme grab a scotch and we can go in the closet," Vivi chortled.

Everyone laughed and it pleasantly broke the building tension. I was actually thankful since I was feeling increasingly awkward. I drew in a deep breath and shook my head. "Well, I sure wish we could. It would certainly relieve some of this angst I feel," I said opening up a bit more.

"Okay spill," Vivi popped. "Who else have you been kissin'?"

"How the hell did you know?" I asked very puzzled.

"Oh, I just know that look of catholic guilt. I grew up looking at myself in the mirror," Vivi surmised.

"Tell us what's happening. I'm sure it's not so bad," Blake added.

I told the girls about Greg and they responded exactly like Annie had. I had the back up I needed. I still felt like I wanted to tell Ben the truth and just come clean but I didn't feel nearly as bad anymore. With Annie, and now the girls, I had the back-up I craved. I felt a little better about myself. Plus I knew if I told Ben it would only stir up trouble and mistrust. They were right; it meant nothing. At least this helped to ease the guilt. I mainly didn't want to hurt Ben for no reason. So I let it go as best I could.

"Okay little drunk-ass ladies, we need to get to planning," Vivi announced. They all giggled as Vivi pulled out her notepad. "Lewis will be home with Tallulah in an hour and I gotta get the notes finished so we have the ball rollin' on the project. I already know who will be catering and decorating."

"Of course!" Blake popped with excitement. "We never do anything without the Fru Fru's."

"Absolutely!" Vivi added with a wide smile. "Never ever! We only want the best and Coco and Jean-Pierre are beyond the best. It will be a shindig of legendary proportions. I will give them a call this afternoon." Vivi looked down and wrote herself a note on the pink planner she was holding.

The Fru Fru's were a catering company and the girls, including my sister Rhonda always used them at huge events. They were hilarious and fantastic at what they did. I was getting excited.

They began fleshing out ideas. I was assigned cupcake duty since Martha May had died. It felt good to be planning for a charity that really needed us. Those ladies in the shelter were like family to Vivi. I swear she was an unexpected role model. But I found myself wanting to be more like her, and knew I would love being around her as we planned the Memorial Day event. It was to be held at the old homestead of my family, Granny Cartwright's, that now was Rhonda's B&B, Southern Comforts. Rhonda was a chef by trade and would be catering the entire affair. It was so exciting. And I was thrilled to be doing something different that had some meaning.

Vivi put on some coffee to offset the earlier drinking and the house filled with the settling aroma of the rich brew. Blake got up to grab some cups and set them all down on the counter as Vivi filled them up for each of us. Blake grabbed them and passed them out to Rhonda and me with a smile that was bright and comforting. Vivi and Blake worked in tandem, better than any old married couple I had ever seen. I watched them as they moved around together as one. It was a sight to see and one to certainly aspire to. They shared a love as deep as the Alabama red clay. I took notice and smiled, thinking of Annie and me. The deep friendships shared by all of us were a kind of sisterhood I was so proud to be part of. It was priceless and rare. I knew I was quieter than Annie and especially Vivi, but I fit here and these women were some of the strongest relationships I had ever built. We took care of each other no matter what. I processed this for a minute and felt the deep comfort and satisfaction it provided. Guilt and worry faded as I sat in Vivi's warm kitchen filled with these special women. It was a moment I would cherish and it would become etched in my memory when I needed to remember how lucky I was.

Just then my cell rang in my purse. I grabbed it off the counter-top from behind me. It was Annie.

"Hey honey I was just thinking about you," I answered.

"Abby, you gotta get home. I have something to show you. Can you be there asap?"

Annie sounded anxious, almost upset. It was unnerving.

"Yes, of course," I responded. "What's wrong? Are you okay?"

"I am but you won't believe what I just found out. Remember the pictures of the Battle Friedman Home? I was just getting a chance to look them over and you won't believe what I see. I can't tell you on the phone, you gotta see it for yourself. I'll meet you at your house in twenty minutes okay?"

"Okay, you're scaring me but I'm on my way."

I hung up and the girls were naturally curious. I filled them in and told them I had to go fast. I made my apologies and told Rhonda I would call her later.

"I'm going up to Ben's parents' house tonight. Ben's horse has qualified for the Derby and she's sick. He's a mess, so I told him I would go."

"Of course you should," Rhonda said. "Just drive safe, sugar and lemme know when you get back. Enjoy this time with his family. This may be the real deal this time, baby."

I smiled at her as I hugged her goodbye. "I hope you're right. I really do."

I was home before I even knew it. Annie was waiting for me in front of my house. She got out clutching her laptop under her arm and walked at a clip to meet me at the porch.

"I cannot believe what I think I found. And honey you won't believe it either." Annie was breathing hard and talking fast. "It is the biggest shock."

"Hurry up. I can't wait any longer," I declared. "It's killing me. What the hell is it? Did you see Bigfoot on the grounds at Battle-Friedman?"

"Haha, very funny Abby. Looka here," she revealed. "Tell me what you see."

Annie had led the way to the kitchen and sat down at my round table with her laptop. She had pulled up a picture of us walking toward the gazebo. "I see our asses. I don't get it," I declared.

Annie zoomed in. I could see myself, Jeannette, and Cate all walking from behind. Still nothing.

"I thought Cate had the camera," I remembered.

"That's right she did," Annie confirmed. But she asked me to take it while she ran to catch up with y'all so she could take a few notes. I thought it would be funny to take some ass shots as you walked far ahead of me. It was supposed to be a joke."

"Okay, not that funny but sometimes I don't get your humor," I snarked. "What am I supposed to be seeing here?"

Annie zoomed in all the way.

"Oh my God!" I yelped. "Is she stealing something from my purse?" I could clearly see Cate's hand reaching inside my bag. "What the hell is she doing?"

"Look closely at her hand. Her fingertips are holding a white envelope, Abby. Don't you see what she's doing?" Annie pushed. "She's dropping the envelope into your bag."

My heartbeat suddenly quickened. I couldn't believe my eyes. I moved closer to the screen and squinted just to make sure. I could see it clearly and knew exactly what she was doing.

"Oh my God! Cate is Secret Sister!"

CHAPTER THIRTY-THREE

I glanced up at the antique clock over my desk. The little room off the front of the house I used as my office was bright with the sunshine of the spring afternoon. To the naked eye, everything looked immaculate and perfectly in its place. Shadows danced along the shiny surface of the hardwood floor. It looked like any other ordinary day.

But it wasn't. I felt the shift, not like the shattering shake of an earthquake. Instead it was subtle, like a sudden dizzy spell that faded as quickly as it began.

Annie had left after talking to me in speedy dialog. She hurried because she didn't want to be here when Ben arrived, leaving it to me to discuss things with him as I saw fit. So in her absence, I was left alone for nearly a half hour—too short to really accomplish anything and too long to be alone with my thoughts—to pick things apart in my mind—this is never a good thing. I can easily get so inside my own head, I need a Xanax to get out, though I had never resorted to such. Hell, I could barely drink two drinks in a row, let alone take anything for nerves and anxiety. Plus, I wanted to be conscious for the long drive up north with Ben.

Thank heavens he was early. I heard his car door slam as he got out and made his way to my front porch. I ran to the front windows that overlooked my porch and peered out at him. He was dressed in dark jeans and a bright white button-down oxford. The white shirt was in stark contrast to his dark wavy hair and tan skin. He was beautiful. His face accented in dark stubble of an unshaven beard. I felt a blanket of comfort fall around me just seeing him approach the house. I suddenly felt such a peace and in my safe place. I knew I could tell him anything and he wouldn't run. Was this what it felt like to trust a man completely and fully? If it was, I was ready. I had never felt this feeling before—to see someone and know my troubles were no match for us together. It was a life-changing moment for me watching Ben come up the front steps and catch me in the window, his grin when he saw me told me everything. He felt the same way I did. Safe. At home.

I flung open the door and grabbed him in a massive bear hug. He returned the affection as he picked me up, both of us in a private web of worry. He with his horse and family and me with my plate-full of nerves. I wrapped both legs around him, kissing him like I hadn't seen him in a month. He was all I needed in the craziness of my life. Ben pulled back as I slid gently down the front of his body touching my tip-toes to the floor.

"God, you are a sight for sore eyes," he whispered still hugging me. "You are just what I needed."

"Oh, Ben, me too," I said. "I couldn't wait to see you too."

He leaned down and kissed me again. In those first few minutes at my front door, I felt another shift. A shaking away from my past issues of trust as my well- built walls began to crumble to allow another person inside.

"You ready?" he asked a painful smile on his face—the worry of his filly evident in his eyes.

"I am. Let me just grab my bags and lock up."

I re-checked Gertrude's food and water, made sure the back door was locked, grabbed my purse from the kitchen table and met Ben back at the front door. He had grabbed my small suitcase from in front of the stairs and was standing like a man with a mission, ready to hit the road. I knew I had so much to tell him but it didn't feel like the time to go into much about me, Cate, and secret sister and especially Greg. Ben was filled with worry. I knew he needed to talk so I told myself that was my job—to listen and be as supportive as he needed me to be. He would be leaning on me and I wanted and needed to be there for him.

I liked being in this position. It made me feel strong. This would be the first crisis Ben and I would face in this new place where we found ourselves—adults madly in love, and acting as a couple, as one. It was a first for me. All of the men I had dated once or twice and every time I had found myself with Greg, nothing had ever felt like this. I knew this was how it was supposed to feel.

Ben tossed my bags in the back and opened my door for me. I slid into his little roadster as he closed the door behind me. He came around to get into the drivers seat and we hit the road north. I moved as close to him as I could, placing the palm of my hand onto his muscular thigh, letting him know I was there for him.

"How is she doing today? Have you heard anything?"

"I talked to mom, Britt actually spent the night with her in the barn last night. Her fever spiked a few times but the antibiotics have her under control this morning. With the race in two weeks, the worry is that she will be too weak and dehydrated."

"But Britt is the best and she is emotionally invested. I know the horse is gonna be okay Ben. We have to believe that."

Ben rested his hand on top of mine and then laced his fingers through mine bringing my hand up to his lips, he kissed the back of my hand and smiled a small smile at me.

"I'm so glad you're with me," he said. "I already feel better with you just sitting right here next to me."

It felt good to be there for him. Still there were so many things I wanted to know—like why he broke it off with

Colleen. I knew now at least that he walked away—so my questions were answered about whether or not he'd still be with her had she not left him, as I had heard. But I had so much more floating around in my head. I wanted the details. But I knew it wasn't the right time. It also struck me that the whole time I was with him all those years ago, I never heard him even mention a godmother.

"Ben," I began. "I was wondering, do you have a godmother named Eleanor?"

"Not that I know of. I never knew anyone at all named Eleanor," he answered. "Why?"

"This very old lady at Book Club was talking about her godson named Ben so I just thought I would ask. No big deal." I tried to blow it off.

I leaned my head over onto his broad shoulder and drew in a deep breath trying to help him relax. My own head swirled with more questions now about Eleanor, but I stayed quiet, trying to keep the atmosphere as diffused as possible until we could get to Ben's filly and he could see her with his own eyes.

The late afternoon sun had slipped behind the horizon as we made the turn on the long dirt road passing under an aging white gate that read Flannigan Farms. A cloud of dust followed behind us like a ghost as the amber light of magic hour cast a yellowish glow in the side mirrors of the little red car. Ben sped down the road in a hurry. He was home. I felt my heart skip knowing I would soon be face to face with his mom. She was a very strong but nurturing woman, short and stout and in charge. She loved her only son fiercely and she was not afraid to show it. She and Ben were bonded as tightly as I had ever known a mother and child to be and it made me both envious and scared at the same time. I wanted and needed her approval but it would be difficult at best to attain her full consent after the way Ben and I had ended things so many years ago. My stomach suddenly was in knots.

Shirley Flannigan came running out of the large stately farmhouse as soon as she heard us, wiping her hands on her apron and waving. She had aged a good bit, her salt and pepper hair pulled back in a short ponytail.

"Ben, I'm so glad you're finally here." She hugged him tightly as he grabbed her, his face buried in the nape of her neck.

"I know, Mama. It's gonna be okay."

"Britt's in the barn. You can go see her."

"You remember Abby—I asked her to come with me."

"Of course I remember Abby—she was almost my daughter in law. Almost." She smiled at me with a tad of sarcasm dripping from her last word as she reached over to hug me. It was a little awkward.

Ben reached for me and grabbed my hand leading the way to the barn. We walked around to the left, then around the side of the house. Bushes and budding camellias lined the pathway. We continued toward the back of the farmhouse. Under a thick canopy of oaks the barn rested in a forest of trees and tall bushes. The setting sun shined a dim spotlight on the barn doors, like an orange glow on a red velvet curtain before the start of a play. Ben was silent as he made his way to the stall at a clip. He was anxious and emotional. I could feel it in the grip of his hand.

"Ben!" Britt exclaimed. "Oh I'm so glad you're here. She's needing her man," Britt said standing and hugging her brother. Britt had become known as a top equine vet in the area. Her specialty was racehorses and that had been her plan even as a young teenager, way back when I had first known this special family. Ben's family farm was only one of a few in Northern Alabama. Most of course were up throughout Tennessee and Kentucky. But Britt made a wonderful living traveling all over horse country. It took me aback seeing her all grown up and doing her thing; saving race horses.

"You remember Abby Harper. I asked her to come with me for the weekend."

"So good to see you again, Abby. Ben will surely need some support. This is his girl you know?" Britt was tall and leggy, trim and fit. Long dark hair fell around her shoulders with bangs swept to the side. She had her hair clipped loosely and low in a side ponytail. She had gorgeous dark blue eyes like her brother. Britt was wearing jeans and boots with a dark navy tee-shirt tucked inside a leather belt. She looked like a horse doctor.

"How is she?" Ben asked nervously.

"She's been really sick, but last night she seemed to turn a corner."

Tears welled in Ben's eyes as he let go of my hand and dropped down on his knees to be face-to-face with his horse. She was lying on her side in a bed of golden hay. Her coat was a warm, dark chestnut color and she had white feet that looked like little socks. Her nose had a few little white freckles. She was just beautiful, so muscular with a shiny coat that glistened in the evening light. Britt had a few tubes hanging from a hook filling her with fluids and antibiotics. It was surreal to see such a stunning creature lying on her side with medical paraphernalia scattered around her.

"Hear that girl, you're gonna be just fine," he whispered. Ben pressed his face to hers and kissed the side of her nose.

"Ben probably hasn't told you but he raised this horse," Britt informed. "She was born in late spring three years ago just as his classes were wrapping up at Alabama. He came home to help with the farm when this little filly picked him out to be her man. She was a runt and her brother kept nudging her away from nursing at their mother. Ben stepped in and put her on a proper feeding schedule, nursing her with a bottle every three hours until she grew big and strong. She's his baby. Look at her."

The horse looked at Ben and squinted her eyes as he nuzzled her nose. She laid her head back as he scratched her neck. It was quite a moment seeing him in this setting. He was strong and nurturing soft and masculine all at once. Ben closed his eyes and rested his head against the filly.

"So what's the prognosis? What was wrong with her?" I

asked Britt.

"She had a flu virus. It's not that uncommon in horses, especially the ones that have to visit other barns and racetracks. But if not treated early it can be deadly. The problem is the timing. Though it looks like she's turned a corner, the race is only two weeks away. She needs to be running every single day. She's losing valuable time on the track."

"But she's on the mend now and I will spell you off here staying with her. Has her fever broken?" Ben was very serious. He had a sudden determined look in his eyes. There was no way he would let his horse miss her chance.

"Still a slight fever but the fluids I've been giving her have really helped. We'll just have to wait it out," Britt sighed. "Mama's got dinner ready and you know how she is. We better get to it."

Ben kissed the horse one last time as he got up brushing off the hay and straw clinging to his clothes. Darkness had fallen and a quiet stillness filled the pathway to the farmhouse as we all made our way back.

Dinner was delicious. Comfort food was the menu for the night, meatloaf and mac and cheese, green beans and cornbread filled the table family-style. Steaming bowls of rich and creamy country cooking hit the spot. Ben's dad, Bob was there and as down-home as I remembered him. You'd never know these people were wealthy. There was no pretentiousness, no pompousness. They were regular folks who just happened to breed racehorses for a living.

Bob and Shirley had built this place from the ground up themselves, Bob turning his family farm into a place to sire horses. They were the kind of people the community would call the salt of the earth. And Ben hadn't fallen far from the tree. I was the idiot who had turned her back and walked away from it all.

After dinner, Ben went back to his girlfriend in the barn while Britt and I cleaned up. His mom helped to clear the table while Bob went into his office just off the kitchen. Everyone was so concerned for their star filly. She was fully a member of the family.

"It's good having you up here after all these years," Shirley said smiling at me. It's been a really long time—you know, since I saw Ben seem so satisfied and happy. I pray y'all can make a go of it this time. At least I'm hopin' so." She nodded her head as she turned and headed upstairs. Britt and I were left alone to chat while we cleaned up the supper.

"She's right you, know," Britt began after her mother had left the room.

"What?" I asked gently.

"Ben. I can see it too. He seems at peace, finally. All those years ago you had made him so happy. Then there were the Colleen years. They were a nightmare."

"Really?" I asked full of curiosity, especially after my run-in with her at Book Club.

"Yeah, Ben was just beside himself," Britt continued as she added soap to the sponge. "She gave him a run for his money. I mean you know Ben. He is good—just one of those good guys who always treats his girl with love and so much respect. And he never suspects the worst. He will see the best in a person until she proves him wrong. And Colleen certainly proved him wrong. They had been sorta on and off for a few years until they got suddenly serious after Colleen visited with us up here. Mama and Daddy and I knew she was up to no good. She saw Ben with a big inheritance and before we knew it they were engaged. And that went on for two more years with her planning the most elaborate wedding—you know like she was royalty. The costs were topping a hundred thousand dollars. It was like a circus. Then one day Ben came home early to find her in bed with that other guy. He was really messed up after that."

Oh my word! He actually walked in on Colleen with someone else. I had no idea. I was suddenly nauseous.

"I feel so bad he went through all that," I commiserated. "He is so good and decent," I said acting like I already knew everything.

"Yeah and Colleen told him it was just sex and she didn't love the guy like she loved Ben, like that was some sorta consolation. I hated that royal bitch from day one but Ben was still licking his wounds from losing you all those years ago. He was trying to believe in something again, ya know? No one could talk to him. He wouldn't listen when it came to Colleen. But we all tried. Then when he caught her he was so devastated."

"Because he really loved her?" I asked hoping Britt could clarify.

"Oh my God, no. He wanted to love her but she is an unlovable bitch," Britt broke into laughter as she closed the dishwasher. "No, it was because he was ashamed. Another failed love affair. Ben actually worried he may never find someone to love him as much as he could love. You know?"

"Well he has now," I promised.

Britt started the dishwasher and turned to me. A look of earnestness etched on her pretty face. "Let's go outside to the swing," she offered.

We walked back through the living room and Britt pushed open the screened door to lead the way to the large spanse of the wide front porch. The wooden double swing was hanging to the left of the porch on the end. Frogs and crickets sang as we sat down and Britt made her heart known to me.

"I hope you mean what you just said, Abby. I mean this time I really hope you're ready. He loves you like he will never love anyone else. He never stopped loving you. This is real for him. Mama and I both can see it in his eyes. He's got the love of his life back and please, if you're not serious, if you just like wanna be friends, please, don't do this to him again. He may not recover."

"Britt, listen to me," I said full of emotion. "I love your brother. This time things are very different. We are both so much older and so settled. It's real this time. I can promise you. And if Ben realizes he doesn't want me, he will have to push me away. It won't be me leaving him again. I feel like I want a life, a full, real life with him. Know that I love him with all I have. I will do anything for him. I have never been this way before—not even all those years ago when we were together."

Britt nodded as I spoke. "Ben's an old soul," she interjected. "I don't have to tell you that. He's been ready for marriage and a family for years. I just hope you both want the same things this time, that's all."

I leaned over and hugged her. I knew she was concerned for Ben. But it was all coming back to me. I had always loved this family like my own. They are easy to love, strong and close knit, and their welcoming open arms are far reaching in this tight little community. They are good souls just like Ben. I watched as Britt left me on the swing to go freshen up before heading back to the barn. I had a rare second chance. And I was so sure of my choices. This time, I knew how I felt. I was no longer a child. I was a woman in love with what may be the best guy on the planet.

I got up and began to walk back toward the barn as I spotted Pleiades and made a wish. For Ben and me, for his baby girl in the barn, and for my own future, to begin anew. I was feeling the change I had wanted so badly. And I wasn't forcing anything. It was all happening on it's own, like a kind of metamorphosis. And I had let go instead of controlling it all and it felt really good for a change.

Ben was lying next to his other girl as I entered the barn, the hay smelling so sweet and fresh. I approached him softly and knelt down beside him, slipping my hands through his thick hair. I was comforting him as he nuzzled the filly.

"Hey, I never knew what you named your girlfriend there," I said smiling trying to cheer him up.

Ben stood up and brushed off the straw. He leaned down and helped me up, then held me against him in a firm long hug. I held him in my arms too. It was such a soft and tender moment. "Her name is Stardust," he said. "I named her after my other favorite girl. We will call her by her full name for the race, Stardust In Dixie. Plus she has those little stars on her nose, see?"

I felt tears well and spill over onto my cheeks. "Of course I remember that name. You made it up for me, baby. But weren't you with Colleen when your little girl here was born?"

"I was, but Abby, Colleen was never you. No one else could be. Stardust, meet Stardust," he said to his baby. Then suddenly she stirred, and before we knew it she was standing, wobbly but standing, as if she was answering Ben's calls.

"Oh my God! See what good luck you are? She's gonna make it! Her fever has broken! Oh Abby, she's gonna make it! Britt, Mama, Y'all get out here, Stardust is standing up! She's gonna be okay!" Ben was crying—I was crying as his Mama and Daddy and Britt all came running. Britt grabbed the stethoscope hanging on the stall door and listened to the chestnut colored racehorse.

"Her heart rate is normal. Her fever has broken! Oh wow, what great news. I'll watch her through the weekend and keep her hydrated but it looks good."

I took in the exciting emotional moment. I knew I was right where I belonged, maybe for the very first time.

Two Weeks Later,
Mother's Day Weekend 2016.
And The Kentucky Derby!

CHAPTER THIRTY-FOUR

It was a gorgeous Saturday in Kentucky! I was beyond excited to wake up in the luxurious hotel next to Ben. It was the day he almost lost a few weeks ago when Stardust was so sick. But today was the day the family had been waiting for—it was Derby Day. It was splendid and I had to pinch myself to believe I was really even there. The excited nerves had our adrenaline pumping at an all-time high. Ben was already in the shower after a quick cup of coffee in our suite of the famous Brown Hotel near Churchill Downs. I had never seen a hotel like The Brown. It totally embodied the old south, full of southern hospitality, and ornate fixtures of the storied past of the Deep South. Like I said, I had to pinch myself. I carefully took my pale pink and black rimmed derby hat out of the hard round box I had carried with me. It was fantastic! Organza with ruffles and tiny black feathers, it was just the embodiment of the Derby. Huge and fancy! Annie had helped me pick it out. It matched perfectly with my pale baby pink linen shift dress and black patent high heels. Pink was a new color for me. I usually chose blue but new things were happening. And I was loving every second.

We all arrived at the famous Churchill Downs racetrack for what they call the fastest two minutes in sports. Ben's parents along with Ben and me took the hotel limo to the track and made our way to the stables. Britt was on hand along with the trainer and the groomer. Stardust stood tall looking every bit the champion they knew she was. So much better than she had been two weeks ago when I saw her so sick at the farm.

"Hey y'all. She's looking good this morning, primed and ready," Britt announced.

"She sure does, hey girl. How's my girl?" Ben cooed at his horse. I suddenly saw the father in him. He would be amazing with kids someday, so gentle. He nuzzled her nose close to his and she butted her head against him. I knew immediately I would always have to defer to Ben's other woman. I smiled at the thought.

"We need to get to the seats," Bob said. "It'll be time 'fore we know it."

Ben kissed his filly. "Good luck sweetheart. I love you no matter what," he said then smiled at Britt giving her a hug. "Here we go," he said, nerves shaking his deep voice. I hugged Britt too as the groomer began brushing the rich brown shiny coat of Stardust. We walked away, Ben slipping his fingers through mine and giving them a squeeze.

"We've had plenty of horses make it to the Derby," Bob explained, but not one that we kept as our own. We're all kinda emotionally attached to this one, especially Ben. You know he nursed her himself."

"It's true Abby. This is *my* horse, *mine*." He smiled proudly. Of course she really belongs to my parents, but they let me feed her and name her. So we share her." Ben grinned and deferred to the two people he loved so much.

We arrived at the seating area for owners. My mind was just blown. We were in the famous Courtyard section. The perfect place for the closest heart-pounding action, the first floor Courtyard was as close as it gets. We would be able to view the champion racehorses as they paraded to the track from the paddock and on their return following the triumphant victory presentation in the Winner's Circle just feet away from where we were sitting! Home to horse owners and trainers, this all-inclusive area also offered a premium open bar, gourmet food buffets and private wagering stations. My mouth would barely close as I gazed around. I still couldn't believe I was here.

A waiter came around serving the famous mint juleps. We all grabbed one and made a toast. My heart was already pounding as Ben raised his glass and began to speak. "To things that change your life—named Stardust." He leaned down and kissed me sweetly on the lips and smiled at me as he clanked glasses with his parents and me, then downed the first swig. It was then, that one of those moments hit home for me— one of those un-named things that only some couples share. No one knew my nickname was Stardust. That was for Ben and me only.

"No matter what, it's gonna be a great day," he continued. "Just finally being here with our own horse and my parents and you, Abby. It's all I could ever want wrapped up in this one afternoon."

We all sat down as the horses began to parade to the starting gate. Stardust was number three. My heart was pounding out of my chest and the race hadn't even started. Ben clutched my hand tight as Stardust passed our area. "There she goes," he said. "There's our girl!"

"It's a dream," Shirley, his mom, boasted.

"We did it," Bob beamed. "I can't even believe it myself if I wasn't seeing it with my own eyes."

The announcer came on the loud speaker introducing the horses and then suddenly the bells rang and the horses were off. Stardust was once a favorite but since she had gotten sick so close to the Derby, almost everyone had counted her out. Everyone except Ben. The horses flew past, dust and dirt flying about in their wake. And around they went. The announcer was going crazy as a thoroughbred from Milwaukee named Northern Lights took the early lead. Stardust was a distant third behind another filly named One Of A Kind. We were all standing and jumping and screaming so loud I could barely hear the announcer. Here they come for the last loop! The announcer was yelling.

"And Northern Lights is in the lead but only by a half length, American Dream is now in second taking that spot away from Stardust In Dixie. One Of A Kind is sneaking up with the challenge into the curve and now Northern Lights comes around from the inside to grab the lead again, American Dream has fallen to fourth but now we see Stardust In Dixie coming up from the outside! We're into the stretch with Northern Lights once again taking the lead, but Stardust in Dixie won't back down, she's challenging Northern Lights as they head home to the finish line, it's gonna be a photo finish as One Of A Kind comes around the pack from the outside but Stardust In Dixie is pushing as hard as she can. She's not giving up. Northern Lights is challenging but here comes Stardust In Dixie with all she's got! It's Stardust In Dixie for the photo finish by a nose! Stardust in Dixie is the winner of the 142nd Kentucky Derby! Jockey Tommy Marshall has won and congratulations to Ben Flannigan, the owner of this surprising heart-stopping finish!"

We were all jumping and yelling and tears were falling and I spilled my mint Julep down Bob's back as I jumped and screamed with joy and excitement. We were all hugging each other and laughing.

"Stardust won! Oh my God, She did it! We did it! But wait, I thought we all registered as her owners, the Flannigan Family remember?" Ben stopped to ask his mom.

"No baby, she is your horse, a hundred percent. She has always been your horse. Congratulations sweetheart! You have a Derby Winner!"

"Hah! Oh my God! I'm in some sorta dream, my Gosh, I can't even believe it!" Ben leaned down and lifted me up in his arms, kissing me and turning in circles over and over. My girl just won the Kentucky Derby! It's perfect!"

We all hastily made our way to the Winner's Circle where

Tommy was atop Stardust. The announcer spoke in all the excitement.

"Almost everyone had counted this girl out. She was sick with flu and dehydrated lying in her home stall back in Northern Alabama just two weeks ago, but her owner knew better. Stardust In Dixie was the runt at birth but Mr. Ben Flannigan believed in her and nursed her into the 142nd winner of the Kentucky Derby. Mr. Flannigan, would you like to say a few words?"

A stunned Ben took the mic. "Thank you. I need to extend my sincere thanks to my family, especially my sister, Britt, the best equine vet in the world, also to the trainers and groomers and everyone involved with the care of Stardust. She's a special horse. But I knew that from the day she came into my life," Ben said wiping a stray tear from his cheek.

The announcer looked at Ben and asked one last question. "Any words of advice to future owners who might be ready to throw in the towel?"

Ben looked at me and grinned. "Never give up on someone you love."

CHAPTER THIRTY-FIVE

Ben and I arrived back to my house just after 2AM. It had been a great day in Kentucky. That was an understatement. Ben and I were on a high and I felt we might never come down. We had a huge dinner back at the fancy historical Brown Hotel before Ben and I hit the road home. Honestly, I hated to leave. It had been a life-changing experience. But I still had the Mother's Day event to pull off. In the last couple of weeks I had handed over some of the final details to Cate. I had hired her full-time after Annie found that all-telling picture but I had decided not to confront her about being my Secret Sister. I wanted to wait until just the right moment and I knew that would be on Mother's Day during the big event. I had received one more note from her; similar to the others promising to be there when I needed her most. It was all still so confusing. Why would she be doing this against her own sister?

Ben and I slipped into bed in the wee hours after the Derby. I had asked him to stay so he could go with me to the big event the next day. I snuggled into bed and the feeling of his warm body next to mine was so satisfying. Ben was a protector. He wrapped his bare muscular arms around me and snuggled into my hair, kissing my head and pulling me close. We were now us. And that had given me a kind of peace I was certain I had never felt. Ben and I just fit. Like this had always been meant to be. It just took me a while to let go and let my own fate appear.

The next morning came before I was ready, but the event began at noon and we had to set up. It was bright and early and all of the mothers would be out and about, with their babies and families on this special day. But Ben was next to me and the bed was soft and warm and it was so very early. Still I made my way to the shower and got ready. We rolled into the parking lot to the side of the historic Battle Friedman Home and got out. Annie was already there with Matt by her side. I saw Cate setting up at the Gazebo where Annie would be broadcasting and Rhonda was there with Jack Bennett, our sport's-talk superstar and former Alabama football player. He was her fiancé now. She was making sure he had everything he needed and enjoying the big day. Rhonda and Jack were planning a big Christmas double wedding at Rhonda's B&B with Annie and Matt. It would be spectacular because the Fru Frus were doing the entire thing.

Looking around, I suddenly felt it was going to be a good day, despite whatever Greg and Colleen were doing just down the street. I actually realized I didn't even care.

I decided to keep a level head and stay focused on the day. *Play it classy*, I told myself, *and you will come out the winner*. I kept saying that to myself over and over as we made sure we were all set up for the big event by noon. I had coordinated these events a hundred times and I knew I had my fly girls, my back-up, right there with me. Annie and now Cate were my teammates and we made a hell of a team.

Blake and Vivi along with their husbands and toddlers were all coming so I knew that no matter what that Greg was going to try to pull, I'd have the help I needed.

"Okay Cate, everything looks fantastic. I'm so proud of you," I gleamed.

"Oh thanks, Annie helped me out and with the assistant producers it really all just fell into place."

"Well, I do appreciate it. Did you see the Derby?"

"Oh my Gosh! Yes!! I was jumping and screaming the entire time. I was so happy for Ben. I had no idea he was the new man you were seeing. Colleen is so stupid. She never really appreciated how special he is. You are one lucky girl, and he is pretty lucky too."

"Why thank you, Cate. I think so myself. Good seeing you again. How are you?" Ben interrupted from behind her as he joined the conversation.

Ben had, at one time, almost been her brother-in-law.

"I'm good but not as good as you! I believe congratulations are in order. Seriously I'm so happy for you Ben. You deserve everything you have, everything." She smiled and leaned over to give Ben a quick hug.

"Thanks Cate, that means a lot." Ben smiled back at her.

Annie ran over and almost knocked me down with a huge embrace. "Oh my Lord, I am so happy for y'all! Oh my heavens, Ben!! Your horse won!! Abby!! You got to be there! I'm just so filled with joy for y'all!" Annie was crazy happy and in her true form. Emotional! Matt walked over to join in and Annie introduced him to Ben. Then Ben and I walked over to check in with Jack at his broadcast station. It was so wonderful for all of us to be together.

Then I saw Mother. She was on the arm of Uncle Ron.

Well it was Mother's Day after all and Toots surely couldn't be without her girls. Uncle Ron, her lover, was the man who actually turned out to be Rhonda's biological father. (But that's another story!)

"Hello my little darlin's. What a day! And we can all spend it together. That just makes me as happy as can be," Toots oozed.

Mother was one of a kind, long and leggy, her dark brunette hair swept up into a French Twist, Mad Men style. She wore a baby blue sleeveless linen dress and long pearls. I had to admit, it was good seeing her so happy. Maybe I had changed. I knew how much my own recent happiness had affected me. It was like I had new eyes.

It was nearly noon and already the lot was filling up as mothers and babies along with husbands began to fill the grounds of the Battle Friedman Home. Annie was in her gazebo and Jack was on the front steps to the right of the door. We had bouncy houses and face painting along with games and even an old-fashioned croquette game set up along the side yard. It was a perfect spring day—that was until the canons went off.

WRBI was broadcasting just down the street and they were obviously reliving the entire Civil War and shooting off canons to signify they were on the air. It was disgusting. I stood in front of Annie and gave her the nod. She opened her mic and we were on the air.

"Happy Mother's Day Tuscaloosa! This is Annie Harper from Saved By The Belle and we're live here at the Historic Battle-Friedman Home celebrating moms all over town. Y'all come on down and join in all the fun and meet me and Sports Star Jack Bennett along with many other big stars here at WRCT. I can't wait to meet y'all so come on over to the gazebo and say hey!"

She continued with her happy, exciting banter then tossed it over to Jack to welcome his listeners. I relaxed and told myself not to worry what Greg and the gang were up to. I actually didn't care. As long as he didn't mess me up, he could have Queen Elizabeth as his guest down there and really it didn't phase me. We had such great things planned for the day and in four short hours it would all be over. I kept telling myself. But I had a feeling in the pit of my stomach that things couldn't possibly go as smoothly as they looked like they would.

Ben was over talking with Matt as I approached Cate. She was running around with her clipboard. I had to say, she had surpassed my expectations.

"Hey so I know we have a pretty big finale planned with that guy whose gonna jump out of the airplane," I reminded.

"Right, it's all on track to begin around 3 o'clock," she confirmed.

"Okay, sounds good. Just keep me posted," I smiled. "You're doing great."

My nerves got the best of me. I wanted to tell her I knew she was secret sister. And how much I had appreciated all those notes. But mostly, why she would be so completely against her sister, Colleen. I knew there was no love lost between them but what had happened for her to be so mad at her that she would work for me and work against her own sister? I had so much to ask her. And still there was the question of Eleanor. I knew Cate didn't know about that but her sister Colleen was the one who received the attack from Cujo, the old woman. I had asked Ben about her being his godmother and he said he never heard of her. There were so many things dangling. I had to just get up the nerve and try again later.

But at the moment I was seeing so much smoke waft into the yard. Those canons wouldn't stop. I was ready to go down there to WRBI and tell that Greg to stop it already! It wasn't Veterans Day for God's sake!

"Abby, some of the kids are in a coughing fit because of all this smoke," Toni Lyn reported. "I don't know what to do."

She was trying to help us out but had arrived late, just in time to see all the smoke floating down the street from the Civil War demonstration at the Jemison House.

I turned to her and affirmed. "Me neither. I can't make them stop."

"But I can," Sonny Bartholomew stepped up.

He was the Chief of Police and Blake's husband. "I am pretty sure they don't have any sort of permits so I can go over there and shut them down. It won't be pretty." He grinned a cock-eyed grin and sauntered across the yard toward the street. Blake stepped up with her 2 ½ year old precious boy on her hip.

"It sure pays to be married to a powerful man. And, it's such a turn-on," she oozed.

"It sure does, and I love it," Vivi popped bragging about being married to Lewis Heart who was the Bama Play-By Play announcer and the owner of our radio station. "We both got us a good man," she added.

"I think we all hit the jackpot," I bragged.

Lewis was running around with a croquet mallet playing with little redheaded Tallulah who was just fixin' to turn three. She was the spitting image of Vivi.

Just then another canon, and this time all the car alarms went off, honking incessantly as dogs started to bark from behind the venue. Between the noise and the smoke it was just ridiculous. My entire event was being drowned out by smoke and noise. I was at my breaking point and was tempted to go down the street and silence that canon by myself. That damn Greg knew exactly what he was doing. He couldn't out-do us so he thought he'd wreck the event instead.

I was standing with Cate right on the lawn between Abby and Jack when I was thumped hard in the back of the head. It nearly knocked me down whatever it was. I turned around and saw a young man in shorts holding one of those huge tee-shirt guns. He was shooting into the crowd.

"Did you hire a tee-shirt shooter," I asked Cate.

"Oh no, I would never do that with all these kids and babies here."

"Exactly! What the hell?" Toni Lyn added.

And then another shot almost hitting Lewis himself. "What the hell was that?" I heard him yell as he ripped Tallulah from the yard clutching her protectively to his broad chest. One of the shirts lay unraveled on the ground. On the front in big letters it read, WRBI. Greg!

I marched right over at a clip toward the shooter and that little shit took off running—and I ran after him, heels and all. All the way down to the WRBI live remote. Greg had hired the T-shirt shooter to advertise his station at our event. That son of a bitch! That was the last straw.

I walked all around the venue looking for him. Under the

main tents and all around the yard. Amazingly, I didn't see Colleen either. I decided to go inside the Jemison Mansion and sneak around. Just then I heard voices in the kitchen. I spied Jamie Walsh, Ben's TA who he had set up to intern there. She put her index finger to her lips signaling me to be quiet and pointed toward the kitchen with a grin. I stopped cold to listen.

"I cannot believe she even got that house. That little slut. The tee-shirt shooters ought to be down there by now. I hope she gets hit. I told the guy what she looked like."

"I know it—I mean I tried like you told me to. I called her and cancelled the damn venue weeks ago but somehow she figured it out. She ain't as dumb as you remembered."

"No but she sure is a little spy herself these days. I'm sure Greg told y'all what she tried to pull with him the other night."

It was three women. I moved to the door facing and peered around the corner. Colleen, Serena and Oh my God—Toni Lyn! She was the station spy! She was their secret agent this whole time! It was them all along!

Just then, "I hope Greg knows, I've tried. He swore if I helped him he wouldn't show those nudy pictures he has of me," Toni Lyn sassed.

Oh my Lord! Toni Lyn was in it with Greg. That's why even though she was our station manager, she had been spying for him.

What do I do? And my true nature came out before I cold stop myself. I have always been fight, not flight. And this little predisposition had always served me well.

CHAPTER THIRTY-SIX

"Well well, hello ladies. How very interesting to find y'all here conspiring together. So nice to see you again. Serena, like my new look? It seems to me you're the dumbass who would fall for a story of plastic surgery to make your long lost friend unrecognizable. And Colleen. Who's really the slut here? C'mon—wasn't it you who your fiancé found in bed with another man? I do believe by anyone's dictionary that would qualify *you* as the slut. And Toni Lyn! You should be ashamed. I guess now you'll be unemployed, and maybe violently attacked once I tell Vivi. Having fun with all this planning and conniving to ruin my event? I sure do hope so. Oh here they are now—come quick and watch. I wouldn't want you to miss this!"

The girls walked slowly over to the large encasement kitchen window just in time to see Sonny out there with Greg.

"Y'all know who that is?"

"The Chief of Police?" Serena answered weakly.

"Oh very good sweetie, you get an A+ in Civics for the day. Y'all have any idea why he's here? Let me help you. He's signing a citation for the canon not being permitted. Guess what he's gonna do next? No idea? Oh well he's gonna come in here and write y'all one too. Watch this."

I knocked on the window and got Sonny's attention. I waved at him and motioned him inside. He tore off the ticket and walked to the back door just off the kitchen.

"What can I do for you, Miss Abby?"

These ladies here falsified a phone call pretending to be a local business in order to deceive a business transaction. That's deception I do believe. Also they have a tee-shirt shooter that they have instructed to specifically aim at a person. I believe that's intent to cause bodily harm. Could you please see that they have their own citations? Thanks so much. Ladies, may I introduce Sonny Bartholomew, the Tuscaloosa Chief Of Police."

I smiled at both of them. "Hmm, not so stupid after all huh?" I walked out the back door and saw Greg. I didn't even bother to waste my time speaking to him. I just looked at him and shook my head and smiled. I had won. And he knew it. I left his little event and walked back up the street to my Mother's Day party.

It was nearly three o'clock so I knew it was almost time for our big finale. But first I knew I had to talk to Cate. She was standing near one of the bouncy houses where she had kicked off her heels and was standing barefoot in white Capri pants and a yellow sweater helping small laughing children in and out of the fun-house. She was smiling and so innocent. I hate that I had so misjudged her.

"Cate can I see you for a quick sec?" I yelled. I motioned to one of the production assistants to go over and relieve her. Cate made her way through the freshly mown grass over to me.

"Can I talk to you for a minute?" I asked with a smile.

"Everything's okay I hope," she answered back nervously.

"Of course, lets go sit down for a minute," I suggested.

We walked inside and up to the parlor and sat down near a big floor to ceiling window to the left of the front door.

After we were both seated and comfortable I looked at her pretty innocent face. Her luminous skin glistened from the perspiration of playing with the children outside.

"Cate, I have to say, you have far surpassed my expectations and I want to apologize for being so distant and doubting you a few weeks ago when you first started with us."

"Oh, Ms. Harper really, I have no idea what you mean. You have been kind from the get-go."

"Please just call me Abby. We're friends now. I wanted to show you a picture. Tell me what you see."

I pulled the picture of her placing a Secret Sister note into my purse from last month. I wanted to see her reaction. I handed it to her as she squinted to look closer at the photo. Then she nearly burst into tears.

"Oh, Ms. Harper, er, uhm , Abby, uh, oh my heavens, I don't even know what to say. I'm so sorry."

"Are you Secret Sister? I know you are from the picture. But why?"

"Oh Goodness, I'm so embarrassed. I just, well I just wanted you to know you had a friend. I mean someday you seemed so overwhelmed and so lost, I just felt so bad for you. And I know just how you felt. I had been there working with my sister all those years in television. She could be so pompous and condescending. I was trying to give you a little boost. That's all."

"You mean you knew all along Colleen was planning to try to undo my event?"

"Well I knew she had always wanted to undo you and everything you were ever trying to create. Ever since she went to work for Greg that was her motivation. She was his spy. She just wants to out do *you,* " she explained.

"But why? She has no reason too."

"Oh yes she sure thinks she does. When she was with Ben he talked about you here and there and it used to make her so jealous. She thought he was still in love with you and she could never compete with the one that got away—you. She has plenty of motivation to try to be your undoing."

I had to take this all in. I leaned back in the soft chintz chair and shook my head. I almost couldn't believe my ears.

Still something didn't make much sense.

"Cate, thank you for telling me but still there's one thing I don't totally understand." I leaned back over toward her. " I can see that you wanted to help me but why? I mean okay she hates me because of Ben, but she's your sister. I know you barely speak these days and you don't really get along but why would you be so loyal to me? How could you be so motivated to side against your own flesh and blood?"

Cate heaved on a deep breath as tears filled her blue eyes. Her bottom lip began to quiver as she shook her head lost in a painful memory.

"So you know why Ben and Colleen broke up?"

"Yes, he walked in on her having sex with someone else while he was engaged to her, right?"

"He walked in on her having sex with my fiancé." The tears slid down her dewy cheeks as she looked at me, obviously still in so much pain.

"Oh my God, Cate. I had no idea. I'm so sorry."

"I'm so sorry too. Ben and I were the collateral damage. Colleen is a bitch. She always was. I had to separate myself from her and go my own way. And you have given me a home here and a place that makes me so proud of myself."

I reached over and hugged her. We both stood up and hugged again. We were sisters. And we both knew it.

"Oh how'd you like Eleanor?" She broke the moment with a smile and wink at me.

"What? Eleanor from Book Club? How do you know about her?"

"She's my neighbor. I paid her a hundred dollars and told her to improv. She was an actress in her youth."

"That's why Ben never heard of her. Godmother? You *are* good!" I hugged her again when suddenly, one of the production assistants ran inside yelling, "Its time, the jumper is over head come quick!"

Cate wiped her tears with her sleeve as we leapt out onto the front porch. Annie and Jack were tag teaming, announcing the finale. Matt had organized the jump through his outdoor store and everyone stood waiting in the front lawn, all eyes peering up into the heavens for the jumper to leap from the airplane and land right in front of us.

All of a sudden, "Oh no!" Matt yelled. "He's headed the wrong way!" He must have gotten confused." Matt, all six feet five of him took off sprinting down the street.

The man was floating down as the crowd yelled *oooooooohhhhhh* simultaneously watching as he floated over the WRBI event.

"Wow, it looks like he's having some trouble," I heard Jack announce over the air.

"He's looks like he's headed to the wrong place," Annie shrieked.

"Oh no! How could this be?" I asked.

"Yep, he's way off course, he's coming down too fast," Lewis yelped.

"Why is that man yelling down there?" I heard a little girl ask her mother.

"Honey, it's all just a show, pretend. Remember?" The smart mother said smirking at me.

We all watched in awe as the jumper headed right for the very center of Greg's illustrious event. My crowd all began to follow the man in the air, moving like a heard of elephants down the street toward where the jumper might land. It was like a slow motion free-fall, with the hoards of people moving as a unit down the middle of the closed Greensboro Boulevard. And then just as we all arrived down the street at WRBI's event,

"Here he comes, he's gonna land on the tent. Oh no!" One lady screamed.

"Watch out! Watch out! Y'all move back," Greg was yelling and running around trying to get the swelling crowd to safety.

Sonny stepped in and Matt and Ben joined him pushing the throngs of event-goers back to safety.

"Watch out, y'all, I'm comin' in hot!" The parachute man screeched as he dropped like a rock straight on top of the main tent and plopped right into the oversized five foot cake as icing flew in every direction. Happy Mothers Day! Well that *was* what it said.

The parachute was slung to the side. The tent had collapsed and everyone was covered in pink cake. I saw Greg on the ground, covered in pink icing. I couldn't help myself.

"Well, I guess you stole the grand finale. Congratulations!" And I blew him a kiss and linked my arm through Ben's as we turned and walked back up the street.

CHAPTER THIRTY-SEVEN

Everything had turned out better than I could have ever hoped. And I felt a hint of Zelda bubbling up as I finished loading the car. She was put away for her insanity, but truthfully she was strong, stubborn to a fault. She never gave up even though in the end many people thought she had lost her mind. I could relate. I loved that she was part of me. She helped me get though this last month. Her determination to fight for what she wanted had been an inspiration and I would forever be grateful. Zelda was like a new sister. She had my back. I smiled as I thought about her and closed the car doors for the night.

The event was over and I stood in the yard of the Battle-Friedman Home proud of what we had pulled together in such a short amount of time—me and all my "sisters."

The clean-up was finished. Ben had stayed with me until the bitter end. We were the last ones still on the grounds as I descended the steps after locking up. I had to return the keys to Jeannette on Monday.

"I know you must be exhausted," Ben said slipping his arm around my waist.

"I sure am but it was all so good. Perfect in fact."

"My mom called and they lost their main PR Director. I

guess she had quit on Friday before the Derby. It was an amicable split. She went to work for the Derby itself. But now we need a great PR director for the Farms. And I only know one. You can stay in town and work from home if you're interested."

"Oh wow, this is really something," I said taken aback. I knew instantly I was more than ready. And I knew I could do a fantastic job, especially since Stardust had just won the Derby. I had to process it but it was really perfect timing. "Let me call her tomorrow and see if they might like to talk to me," I offered.

"Oh they want to talk. Believe me," Ben affirmed.

"And I could work from home?" I asked to make sure.

"Yep," he answered with a grin. Either home, you know, mine or yours."

I smiled at him and meandered over to the gazebo and took a seat on the bench inside. I gazed up at the stars overhead. The darkness of the velvety night sky made for a perfect night to look to the heavens and find my little cluster. I found it surreal that here we were again, back in a gazebo together, just like when Ben had once proposed to me. I smiled at the distant memory.

"Do you see it?" Ben asked.

"There it is, faint and sweet just to the right of Orion. My Pleiades."

"Close your eyes and make a wish," he whispered.

I did. I smiled to myself as I pictured Ben and me taking part in a Mother's Day event of our own, our babies toddling around in their Sunday best. I wished for a life with him. It was all I wanted now. Nothing else seemed to matter to me anymore.

I opened my eyes to see my beautiful sweet Ben down on one knee, his adorable smile and wide anxious eyes gazing up at me. And in his palm a small blue velvet box. I opened it to see a perfect cushion cut antique diamond ring set in surrounding diamonds. It glistened in the moon shadows catching the light as I pulled it toward me.

"Abby, I love you. I have loved you most of my life. I never give up on someone I love. I want to spend this lifetime with you and make you happy. I want you to annoy me with all your incessant cleaning. There is no one else for me but you. I want to be your wish upon the stars. Please make me the happiest, luckiest man on earth and do me the honor of marring me. Will you marry me Abby?"

"Oh Ben, it was my wish tonight. I wanted a life with you! Yes! Yes! I will marry you! Yes!" I slid off the bench and down onto Ben's waiting lap and kissed him over and over. I was so filled with joy, I was crying happy tears. "And I am so thrilled to annoy you too—for the rest of my life." I giggled.

"I'm so happy this gazebo was a little luckier than the last one," he laughed holding me close.

"Maybe we can join my sister's and get married at Christmastime! A triple wedding!" I felt like I needed to pinch myself. Was this my life? I couldn't remember being so happy, maybe ever.

It was the most perfect night of my life. Under a canopy of a jillion stars, in the arms of the man I loved, the man I had always loved. He slipped the stunning ring onto my finger and perfectly it caught the moonlight with a sudden sparkle. My life had taken a turn and for once I had stopped trying to control it. What bliss I had found in the unplanned, unexpected world of chance. Annie was right. *Let go so your life can find you.* I did.

And it had.

The End

EPILOGUE

Ben and I drove home together under the cloudless starry sky. As we made the turn into the driveway, we both saw it and laughed out loud.

Mitzy had a sign in her front yard.

For Sale.

Dear Reader,

I wanted to take this space to acknowledge YOU. I want you to know that from the bottom of my heart, I know that you make me what I am. Nothing pleases me more than hearing from all of you and the best thing is to get to meet you, give you a big hug and thank you in person for buying my books, and laughing, and letting me know you're laughing.

Some of you are going through personal struggles and challenges and you have been so wonderful to let me know that my books help keep your spirits up and keep you smiling. My all time favorite thing to hear was when someone gave a review saying, "Don't ever read a book by Beth Albright with anything in your mouth unless you love doing a spit-take." That made me giggle! And made me really happy!

A moment that still gives me chills and brings a tear to my eye was when I met a reader at the Barbara Vey Readers Appreciation Luncheon, (My all-time favorite event every year) who actually quoted me—to me! I loved hearing how something a character said made her laugh hysterically then stick with her. My job is done. That is all I wish for—to make you happy, make you feel, or think or cry or fall in love. And especially to laugh.

So I want to acknowledge YOU, dear readers, and many of you have now become my personal friends, which I love, for supporting me and helping me to spread the word about all of my books. You give me so much in return! You can't imagine how you warm my heart. Love to all of you!!

Beth

MEET BETH ALBRIGHT

 Beth Albright is a Tuscaloosa native, former Days Of Our Lives actress, and former radio and TV talk show host. She is a graduate of the University Of Alabama School of Journalism. She is also a screenwriter, voice-over artist, wife of her college sweetheart, Ted and mother of her favorite person on earth, her brilliant handsome son, Brooks. A perpetually homesick Southern Belle and a major Alabama Crimson Tide fan, she splits her time between Phoenix, Arizona and, of course, Tuscaloosa.

Beth loves to connect with her readers.

Visit her online:
www.bethalbrightbooks.com

Facebook:
https://www.facebook.com/authorbethalbright

Twitter:
https://twitter.com/BeththeBelle

Goodreads:
https://www.goodreads.com/author/show/
6583748.Beth_Albright

Made in the USA
Lexington, KY
22 October 2016